Cyclades

GREECE

EVIA

CHIOS

Athens

Andros

KEA   TINOS   IKARIA

Syros   Mykonos

Delos

Paros   Naxos

MILOS   Ios

KITHIRA   Santorini

Aegean Sea

CRETE

HarperCollins*Publishers*

This book was produced using QuarkXPress™ and
Adobe Illustrator 88™ on Apple Macintosh™ computers
and output to separated film on a Linotronic™ 300 Imagesetter

Text: Paul Murphy
Photography: Monica Wells
Cartography: Susan Harvey
Design: Lynsey Roxburgh

First published 1991
Copyright © HarperCollins Publishers
Produced by Collins Manufacturing, Glasgow
ISBN 0 00 435761-2

HOW TO USE THIS BOOK

Your Collins Traveller Guide will help you find your way around your holiday destination quickly and easily. It is split into two sections which are colour-coded:

The blue section provides you with an alphabetical sequence of headings, from **BEACHES** to **WALKS** via **EXCURSIONS**, **NIGHTLIFE**, **RESTAURANTS**, etc. for the main islands in the Cyclades. Each entry within a topic includes information on how to get there, how much it will cost you, when it will be open and what to expect. Furthermore, every page has its own map showing the position of each item and the nearest landmark. This allows you to orientate yourself quickly and easily in your new surroundings. To find what you want to do – having dinner, visiting a museum, going for a walk or sightseeing – simply flick through the blue headings and take your pick!

The red section is an alphabetical list of information. It provides essential facts about places and cultural items – 'What is a Kouros?', 'When is the Siesta?', 'Where are the Little Cyclades?' – and expands on subjects touched on in the first half of the book. This section also contains practical travel information. It ranges through how to find accommodation, where to hire a car, the availability of camping facilities, the variety of eating places and food available, tips on health, information on money and how to find a taxi. It is lively and informative and easy to use. Each band shows the first three letters of the first entry on the page. Simply flick through the bands till you find the entry you need!

All the main entries are also cross-referenced to help you find them. Names in small capitals – **MYKONOS-BEACHES** – tell you that there is more information about the item you are looking for under the topic on beaches on Mykonos in the first part of the book. So when you read 'see **MYKONOS-BEACHES**' you turn to the blue heading for **MYKONOS-BEACHES**. The instruction 'see **A-Z**', after a word, lets you know that the word has its own entry in the second part of the book. Similarly words in bold type – **Amorgos** – also let you know that there is an entry in the A-Z for the indicated name. In both cases you just look under the appropriate heading in the red section.

Packed full of information and easy to use – you'll always know where you are with your Collins Traveller Guide!

Aegean Sea

AGIOS PROKOPIOS

AGIOS GEORGIOS

Galini

Engares

Naxos
Town

Glinado

Galanado

MIKRI
VIGLA

Ano
Sangri

Cape
Mikri
Vigla

KASTRAKI

PYRGAKI

INTRODUCTION

n ancient times the group of islands which lay around Delos, that Aegean holy of holies, came to be known as the Kyklades, meaning 'the encircling islands'. Some 2500 years later the configuration and the name remain the same but the centre has shifted, ever so slightly, 2.5 nautical miles northeast. The new sacred island is Mykonos. While Delos is now a ruin, populated by headless statues

and a handful of archaeologists, the beaches, streets and bars of its neighbour are thronged with bronzed hedonists. These playboys and playgirls (though on Mykonos the distinction blurs) of the Western world come to worship the new god, Leisure. And indeed Mykonos is the quintessential Cycladic island: a small, barren rock dotted with tiny settlements and fringed with sandy beaches, it suddenly clusters glori-

ously together in its Chora, Mykonos Town. Imagine a brilliant-white labyrinth of cubic houses set off by red-roofed churches, sky-blue doors, bright green window frames, yellow balustrades and a riot of bougainvillea, hibiscus and geraniums. It could only be Mykonos – or Naxos, or Paros, or any one of several Choras in the Cyclades. But nowhere is it more beautiful than Mykonos: they even have windmills and pelicans. There are 24 inhabited islands (excluding Delos) in the Cyclades. The smallest, Epano Koufonissi, is just 5 sq km (less than the size of a small town), and on its deserted neighbour, Ano Koufonissi, you could live the life of Robinson Crusoe. The largest, Naxos, at 428 sq km, is the most complete of the Cyclades, offering wonderful beaches, dramatic, verdant mountain scenery and an atmospheric medieval Chora. Most importantly it has developed to accommodate visitors without losing its charm. Catch it while you can, before the airport is built there.

The islands fall, more or less, into one of four categories. Firstly, there are those which have been developed to service the north- and west-European market. In the past they were predominantly the preserve of young independent travellers but with the advent of island airports they have come to cater for a broader range of tourists. These include Mykonos, Paros, Naxos, Ios and Santorini. But although Naxos and Ios are only a few nautical miles from each other, as far as the type of

visitor they attract is concerned, they are oceans apart. And this is true throughout the Cyclades: each island is similar, yet has its own character and its own atmosphere. The second category comprises those islands developed as Greek holiday-makers' resorts and includes much of the eastern Cyclades: Kea, Kithnos and Sifnos. These are more family-orientated than the western Cyclades. Those islands in the throes of being developed, or already having a small tourism infrastructure, include Andros, Amorgos, Folegandros and Milos. And finally there are those islands largely untouched by tourism: Anafi, Serifos, Sikinos and the Little Cyclades.

By definition these categories are broad generalizations and you may find more life in Adamas on Milos than anywhere on Kea or Kithnos. Sifnos may also dispute the above category as it is becoming increasingly popular with British holiday-makers. The term 'developed' must also be understood in its context with regard to the Cyclades. Here, thank goodness, there are no high-rise blocks and few 'holiday complexes'. Public transport is an adventure rather than a simple logistics exercise, and a meal in a crowded, basic taverna is a world away from the sanitized dining experience in a Costa hotel.

Even on tourist-rich Mykonos you can still see the farmer and his yoked cattle struggling to plough a rustic furrow in the unlovely, barren earth. For those who live here and do not feed off the hand of tourism, this is a hard life. You can see it in the decaying rural houses and hill villages, you can see it in the vast number of churches (built as thanks to God for deliverance from the meltemi-tossed seas) and you can see it most clearly in the weather-beaten faces of the old folks. Even your friends at home can see them, captured on picture postcards with 'greetings from Paros' or wherever. It's a wonder in many ways that the islanders are so open and friendly, and a tragedy that some tourists push their honesty and ingenuity to the limit. Fortunately, with the dishonourable exception of Ios, the Cyclades have not yet gone the way of Corfu or of Lindos on Rhodes, and the vast majority of islands and settlements have kept their local culture.

The best time to visit the Cyclades is most definitely out of the high season. In July and August the swarming crowds can totally eradicate the charm of tiny streets and settlements designed for one-tenth that number of people moving at one-tenth of that speed. Aside from beach activities there is relatively little to do or see on most islands, so island-hopping is the norm. However, it may take you longer than anticipated to travel around, so don't try to cram too many destinations into your stay. Four islands in two weeks or six in three weeks is probably a comfortable limit. On the eastern chain Santorini is stunning (but lacks

beach appeal), Paros and Naxos are ideal for first-timers, Andros, Syros and Tinos will appeal to confirmed Graecophiles, and Mykonos is – just Mykonos. The western islands are less accessible as inter-island connections are not so good, there is less route flexibility (as they really are a north-south chain) and they cater mostly for Greek tourists. However, a combination of Milos, Kimolos and Serifos should satisfy most Greek-minded travellers. There is also a direct link from Paros to Sifnos.

The Cyclades have traditionally been the haunt of independent travellers and you will encounter young backpackers everywhere. Making your own way, though not necessarily under canvas, is still the best way of experiencing the real island flavour and unless you have a young family in tow or are particularly selective about the type of accommodation you want, you will have, as the Greeks are fond of saying, 'no problem'. Just take along an open mind, plenty of suntan lotion and this guidebook.

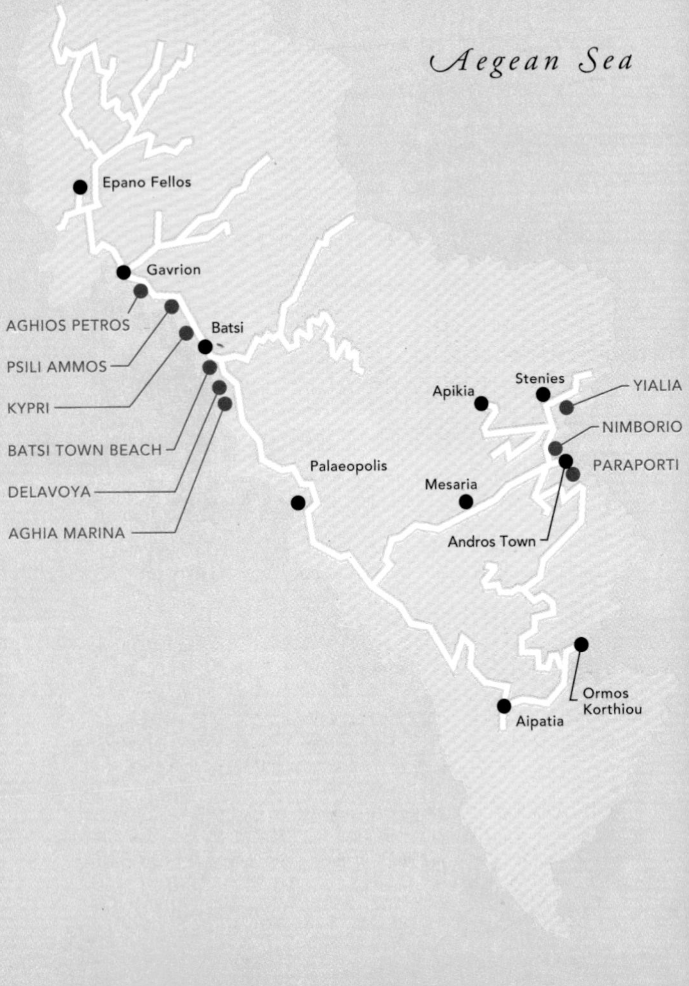

Aegean Sea

Epano Fellos

Gavrion

AGHIOS PETROS

Batsi

PSILI AMMOS

KYPRI

BATSI TOWN BEACH

DELAVOYA

AGHIA MARINA

Apikia

Stenies

YIALIA

NIMBORIO

PARAPORTI

Palaeopolis

Mesaria

Andros Town

Ormos Korthiou

Aipatia

AGHIOS PETROS 1.75 km south of Gavrion, 5.25 km north of Batsi. Bus from Gavrion or Batsi.
A long stretch of coarse and fine sand; no shade. Taverna and pizzeria.

PSILI AMMOS 2.25 km south of Gavrion, 4.75 km north of Batsi. Bus from Gavrion or Batsi.
Beautiful, small, fine-sand cove in protected corner of bay. No facilities.

KYPRI 2.5 km south of Gavrion, 4.5 km north of Batsi. Bus from Gavrion or Batsi.
Long, open, coarse-sand and pebble beach lying adjacent to the main road. Little shade nearby but there is one restaurant at Pell Mell disco.

BATSI TOWN BEACH Batsi.
A beautifully situated half-km sweep of coarse sand next to the picturesque fishing port of Batsi. Windsurfing, pedaloes and canoes.

DELAVOYA 1 km south of Batsi. Water taxi from port.
Picturesque, small, fine-sand cove at the bottom of steps overlooked by Aneroussa Beach Hotel. Little shade; popular with nudists.

AGHIA MARINA 1.5 km south of Batsi. Water taxi from port.
Small, narrow, sandy beach serviced by one taverna. Little shade.

PARAPORTI Andros Town Beach – south.
Wide and wild stretch of grey sand some half km long, backed by dunes and bushes. Usually a quiet beach, with little shade and no facilities.

NIMBORIO Andros Town Beach – north.
This long, narrow strip of greyish sand stretching round its protected bay is popular with locals and families. Tavernas and bars on the road.

YIALIA Stenies, 5 km north of Andros Town. Bus from Andros Town.
Shaded by trees and protected by a rocky headland, this is a pleasant sand-and-pebble beach. Facilities include a restaurant and windsurfing.
See **ANDROS-EXCURSION**.

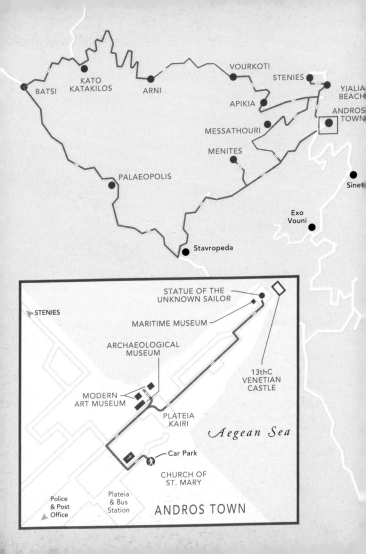

KATO
KATAKILOS

BATSI

ARNI

VOURKOTI

STENIES

YIALIA
BEACH

APIKIA

ANDROS
TOWN

MESSATHOURI

MENITES

PALAEOPOLIS

Sinet

Exo
Vouni

Stavropeda

STENIES

STATUE OF THE
UNKNOWN SAILOR

MARITIME MUSEUM

ARCHAEOLOGICAL
MUSEUM

13thC
VENETIAN
CASTLE

MODERN
ART MUSEUM

PLATEIA
KAIRI

Aegean Sea

Car Park

CHURCH OF
ST. MARY

Police
& Post
Office

Plateia
& Bus
Station

ANDROS TOWN

Excursion

*A one-day round-island excursion from Batsi, taking in Andros Town.
See* **Andros***.*

Take the gently climbing coast road south out of Batsi.

8 km – Palaeopolis. This pretty hillside village stands on the site of the old capital town of Andros (destroyed c.AD 500). The ancient submerged harbour jetty is still visible from the road. There is a long descent to a small, pebbly beach. Turn left off the main road to Menites (badly signposted).

21 km – Menites. Take the lower right-hand fork to this small, picturesque village and its famous mineral springs which gush from a wall below the church. Return to the main road.

25 km – Andros Town. Follow signs to the centre, pass the bus station and park by the Church of St. Mary. See the lovely mural-covered interior of the church, built in 1905 (see **Customs**). Go down the steps, turn right and walk 100 m to the main square, Plateia Kairi. A path descends right to the excellent Modern Art Museum (1000-1400, 1800-2000 June-Sep., 1000-1400 Oct.-May; closed Tue. Free unless a special exhibition is on). The building on the right comprises eight small galleries of paintings, prints, drawings and photos, while the

branch on the left features three-dimensional pieces, including 'Musical Instruments' – magnetically controlled pendulums striking tuned wires at random to produce an amazing cacophony. Return to the square to the Archaeological Museum (0845-1500 Mon., Wed.-Sat., 0930-1430 Sun. & hol. 200 Drs). This is a well-presented display of the history and culture of Andros, dating from the Bronze Age to the 18thC. Don't miss the statue of Hermes, winged messenger of the gods (early 1stC AD), found at Palaeopolis. From Plateia Kairi walk through the archway to the end of the peninsula. The huge statue of the Unknown Sailor looks out over the ruins of the early-13thC Venetian castle (see **Venetians**). There is a small maritime museum behind the statue (1000-1300, 1800-2000 Mon., Wed.-Sun. Free).

Return to your vehicle and follow the beach road north. At the end of the beach turn left inland and, after 4 km, right towards Stenies. The road descends into a beautiful cypress-lined verdant valley.

32 km – Yialia. See ANDROS-BEACHES. The same tree-shaded river which runs here also flows further inland, in an almost English country setting, through Stenies, which is reputed to be the richest village on Andros and a holiday home for many wealthy seamen and shipowners. Return to the main road and turn right to Apikia (Sariza).

37 km – Apikia. Like Stenies, this is a wealthy, hillside village with moneyed maritime connections. From here you can either continue through Apikia to return to Batsi by the bumpy, tortuous, spectacular route via Vourkoti and Arni (Arnas) or you can retrace

your journey. Arni is 30 km further on (see below).

If you choose to return the way you came there is a right turn to Messathouri about 2 km from Apikia. Pass through the village and take the rough track on the left for about 1 km before turning right to rejoin the Andros-Batsi road. It is 25 km to Batsi. The total round trip is 67 km.

67 km – Arni. A lovely small village spread prettily below the peak of Profit Ilias, 995 m high. Springs flow all year round making this the lushest spot on the island. From here it is 14 km to Batsi via another lovely unspoilt village, Kato Katakilos. The total round trip is 81 km.

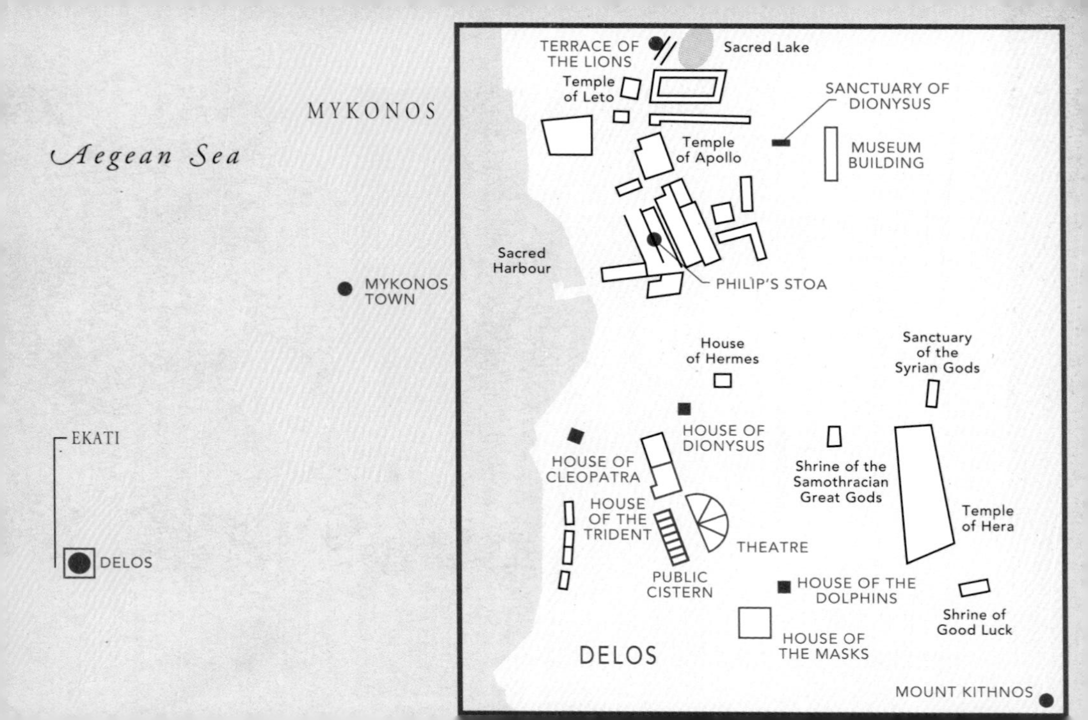
Aegean Sea
MYKONOS
MYKONOS TOWN
EKATI
DELOS
TERRACE OF THE LIONS
Sacred Lake
Temple of Leto
SANCTUARY OF DIONYSUS
Temple of Apollo
MUSEUM BUILDING
Sacred Harbour
PHILIP'S STOA
House of Hermes
Sanctuary of the Syrian Gods
HOUSE OF DIONYSUS
HOUSE OF CLEOPATRA
Shrine of the Samothracian Great Gods
HOUSE OF THE TRIDENT
Temple of Hera
THEATRE
PUBLIC CISTERN
HOUSE OF THE DOLPHINS
Shrine of Good Luck
HOUSE OF THE MASKS
DELOS
MOUNT KITHNOS

Excursion

A one-day excursion from Mykonos (see A-Z) exploring the historic island of Delos (see A-Z).

The best way to see Delos is with a tour guide. However, if you don't want to, or can't get a guide, the following list highlights the main sights. The museum, which is shown on the map, is also well worth a visit if you have time. As it is impossible to cover all the sights of the island properly in one trip, you may well choose to return on your own after a guided tour. If you are considering doing so, ask the gatekeeper to sign the back of your ticket and you will not have to pay the 500 Drs admission to the island if you return the following day.

A typical tour, which includes the ferry trip from Mykonos Town, admission to Delos and the services of a guide, costs 3000 Drs, arriving on the island at 1000 and departing at 1330. If you want to do the tour independently, the ferry costs 750 Drs and admission to the island costs 500 Drs. The first ferry leaves Mykonos Town at 0830 (30 min journey) and the last one departs from Delos at 1330. If you charter your own boat you can arrive at 0830 and stay until 1500 but you must then leave the island.

House of Cleopatra: This Cleopatra was an Athenian. The headless statues, which are copies, are Cleo and her husband standing guard over a small dolphin mosaic.

House of Dionysus: The columns of the open-air courtyard are still intact but time has been less kind to the mosaic depicting Dionysus, god of wine and bounty, on a tiger.

House of the Trident: Once one of the biggest and most luxurious of Delian houses, with dolphins, anchors and tridents featuring in its fine mosaic.

Theatre and Public Cistern: The theatre (c.300 BC) could hold some 5500 spectators. It also helped save water, with rain running off it into the cistern.

House of the Masks: This house contains one of the best mosaics, once again depicting Dionysus, this time riding a panther side-saddle.

House of the Dolphins: Intertwined dolphins reined by Eros, the god of love, feature on a splendid floor.

Mount Kithnos: Although only 123 m high, the view from the summit is

held to be one of the best in the Cyclades, and many of the other
islands can be seen from here.

Stoa of Philip of Macedonia: The blocks which once were on top of the
colonnade lining this processional route are still marked with the
inscription of Philip of Macedonia, who was the father of Alexander the
Great.

Terrace of the Lions: Originally numbering 16 or 18 strong, these
marble beasts may have been an offering from Naxos (see **A-Z**), given
in the 6th-7thC.

Sanctuary of Dionysus: The now-vanished gateway to the Sanctuary
was supported by two giant erect phalluses, the bottom sections of
which still remain.

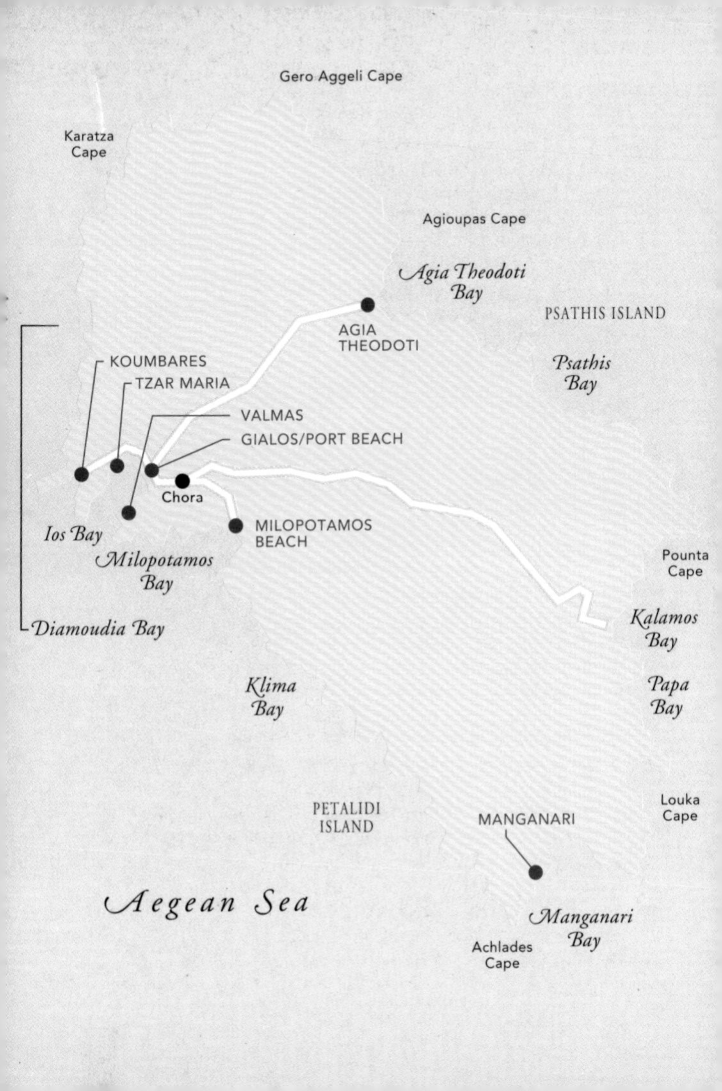

Gero Aggeli Cape

Karatza
Cape

Agioupas Cape

Agia Theodoti
Bay

PSATHIS ISLAND

AGIA
THEODOTI

Psathis
Bay

KOUMBARES
TZAR MARIA

VALMAS
GIALOS/PORT BEACH

Chora

MILOPOTAMOS
BEACH

Pounta
Cape

Ios Bay

Milopotamos
Bay

Kalamos
Bay

Diamoudia Bay

Papa
Bay

Klima
Bay

Louka
Cape

PETALIDI
ISLAND

MANGANARI

Aegean Sea

Manganari
Bay

Achlades
Cape

Beaches

KOUMBARES 2 km west of Gialos. 25 min walk from Gialos.
Small, sandy beach strewn with large pebbles (which are useful for con-structing wind shelters) and set amidst rocky coves. There is some nud-ism here. The waters are good for swimming and snorkelling. There are two tavernas off-beach.

TZAR MARIA 1 km west of Gialos.
15 min walk from Gialos (steps lead down to beach from main track).
Lovely, small, secluded, sand-and-shingle beach cove with excellent swimming. Some nudism; no facilities or refreshments.

GIALOS/PORT BEACH Gialos.
Golden sandy beach some half-km long, backed with trees, tavernas and restaurants. Its shallow water is good for children and novice windsurfers (two windsurfing schools here are English-run). Pedaloes and canoes.

VALMAS 2 km southwest of Gialos. 20 min walk from Gialos.
The small, shingle beach of a long, narrow, protected bay. There is excellent swimming and snorkelling here. One taverna.

MILOPOTAMOS BEACH 2 km south of Chora.
Frequent buses from Chora.
A magnificent 1-km sweep of coarse, golden sand. There are noisy and crowded cafés and bars at the bus-stop end of the beach, but the far end is quieter and popular with nudists. All water sports.

MANGANARI 12 km southeast of Chora.
50 min by boat from Gialos. ❏ 1000 Drs return.
Six lovely, small, silvery sand beaches set in a large, protected bay. Good facilities for refreshment comprise two restaurants, tavernas, bars and a smart hotel complex.

AGIA THEODOTI 8 km east of Chora.
30-45 min by motorbike or moped on non-asphalt road; 45 min by bus. ❏ 1000 Drs return; enquire at Acteon Travel Agency in Chora.
Large, sandy beach in wide bay; good swimming. Tavernas in village.

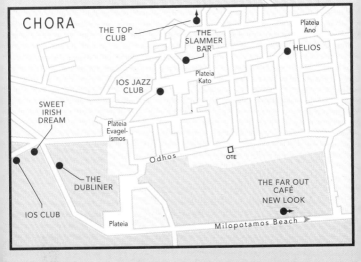

IOS JAZZ CLUB Off Plateia Kato, Chora.
This cosy, candlelit cocktail bar serves alcoholic milk-shake specialities and plays loud jazz and blues.

HELIOS Near Plateia Ano, Chora.
The classiest, most civilized cocktail bar in Chora, Helios has a classic whitewashed bar room with a small, romantic balcony.

THE SLAMMER BAR Near Plateia Kato, Chora.
The place to try an authentic Ios 'Slammer' – tequila, Tia Maria and lemonade – but be careful, as it's powerful stuff!

THE TOP CLUB Up the hill to the top of Chora.
Worth the climb to the top of the village. Enjoy the view over a drink, coffee or a delicious snack, then (from 2300) dance around the palm tree to the latest club sounds.

SWEET IRISH DREAM Next to the steps to Gialos, Chora.
A popular nightspot above the port where you can eat upstairs and dance and drink downstairs.

IOS CLUB Next to the steps to Gialos, Chora.
A pleasant bar famous for its mini amphitheatre where a crowd gathers in the early evening to watch the sunset to the strains of classical music.

THE DUBLINER Near the steps to Gialos, Chora.
Popular with those in the know – a genuine Irish bar where the 'crack' and the partying go on late into the night.

NEW LOOK 100 m outside Chora on road to Milopotamos.
One of Ios's most popular discos, this open-air venue plays New Wave dance music (house, acid, hip-hop, etc.).

THE FAR OUT CAFÉ Milopotamos Beach.
As the name suggests, a latter-day hippy and beach-bum haven. An early-evening video programme plays to a raucous crowd.

Gero Aggeli Cape

Karatza
Cape

Agioupas Cape

*Agia Theodoti
Bay*

PSATHIS ISLAND

*Psathis
Bay*

Ios Bay

CHORA

CHORA

Plateia
Ano

Plateia
Kato

KORALI
THE FISHERMEN

Plateia
Evagelismos

Odhos

OTE

RESTAURANT
CALYPSO

PITHARI

MARCO POLO

VESUVIO PIZZERIA

ROMANTICA ZACHAR

Plateia

Milopotamos Beach →

Restaurants

RESTAURANT CALYPSO Odhos, Chora.
❏ Moderate.
Greek menu with good specials, e.g. souvlakia in pepper sauce (see **Food***); friendly service. Dine in the roof garden or on the pretty terrace.*

MARCO POLO Small cul-de-sac opposite Commercial Bank, Chora.
❏ Moderate.
Pleasant small restaurant set in cul-de-sac with vine-covered terrace. The standard Greek/international menu (see **Food***) also offers some specials.*

VESUVIO PIZZERIA Off Plateia Kato, Chora.
❏ Moderate.
A predominantly Italian menu with good pizzas and lots of pasta served in a bright, cheerful, downstairs room and small, well-lit roof garden.

KORALI Gialos beach.
❏ Moderate.
This hotel restaurant serves incongruous international dishes (like pork in paprika, curries, and French onion soup) on a patio overlooking the beach.

THE FISHERMEN Gialos.
❏ Moderate.
A highly regarded, family-run, basic taverna with a harbour terrace. Fresh fish caught by the family is always available.

ROMANTICA ZACHAR Odhos, Chora.
❏ Inexpensive.
The pretty, rear terrace with hibiscus- and vine-covered bamboo shade makes a nice setting for a relaxed snack or light meal in the early evening. The menu is limited but the pizzas are good and the staff friendly.

PITHARI Plateia Evagelismos, Chora.
❏ Inexpensive.
Generally agreed to serve the best traditional Greek food (see **Food***) on Ios. Eat in a modern, spotlessly clean dining room or outside on the pavement. The head chef is a veteran of 20 years' cooking on a cruise liner.*

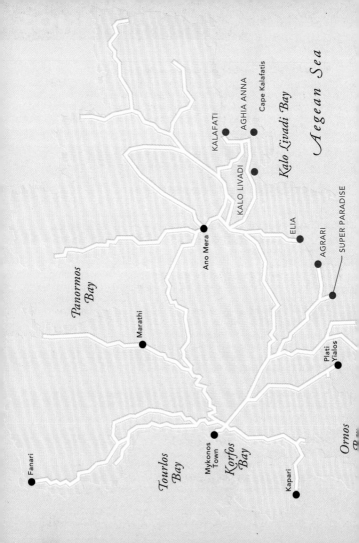

KALAFATI 12 km east of Mykonos Town. No bus.
The most developed of all the southeast beaches, pleasantly overlooked by a church, a windmill and a dovecote (see A-Z). The long, straight, coarse-sand beach is backed by trees and a taverna. Sunshades are available. Recreational facilities include volleyball, water-skiing, wind-surfing and pedaloes.

AGHIA ANNA 11 km east of Mykonos Town. No bus.
Small, coarse-sand and shingle beach set across a little peninsula from a tiny fishing hamlet. Good for swimming. Shade and refreshment can be had in the only taverna.

KALO LIVADI 10 km east of Mykonos Town. No bus.
Long, secluded, quiet stretch of coarse sand set in an undeveloped bay and offering little shade. One taverna provides the only refreshment. Windsurfing and pedaloes.

ELIA 8 km southeast of Mykonos Town.
30 min by bus; 40 min by boat from Plati Yialos.
A lovely broad, long, coarse-sand beach backed by a hillside and one taverna. A good area for swimming and there is a floating platform for diving. Elia is next to Agrari beach (see below).

AGRARI 8 km southeast of Mykonos Town.
30 min by bus; 40 min by boat from Plati Yialos.
Small, coarse-sand beach separated from the adjacent Elia (see above) by a small headland. Swimming is good here, with one taverna providing shade and refreshment.

SUPER PARADISE 5 km southeast of Mykonos Town.
25 min by boat from Plati Yialos.
200 m of lovely, coarse, golden sand in a small bay flanked by large rocks. Nudity is the norm here, although this beach is often misrepresented as being exclusively gay. A cocktail bar and a taverna offer refuge from the rigours of sunbathing. Sunshades are available.

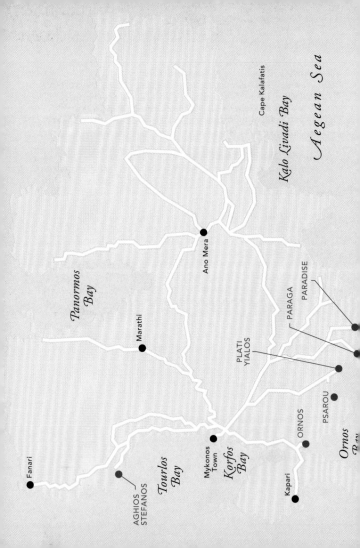

PARADISE 5 km southeast of Mykonos Town.
10 min by boat; 20 min walk from Plati Yialos.
Lovely sweep of coarse, golden sand in a gently curved bay with a rocky backdrop. The reef close to shore is good for snorkelling and diving although it does make swimming awkward. The camping site here has a lively taverna. Scuba-diving; more water sports are planned.

PARAGA (PIRANGA/PARAGKA) 5 km south of Mykonos Town.
5 min by boat from Plati Yialos (check first, as not all boats stop here).
Small bay with large granite slabs enclosing its pretty little coarse, white-sand beach. Two tavernas; sunshades are available.

PLATI YIALOS 3.5 km south of Mykonos Town.
Frequent buses from Mykonos Town.
Pleasant, but the busiest beach on the island as it is the ferry terminus for the popular southern beaches. 200 m of coarse sand covered with shades and sunbeds. Restaurants, bars, tavernas; water-skiing, jet-bikes.

PSAROU 3 km south of Mykonos Town.
Frequent buses from Mykonos Town.
Attractive, popular beach in a sheltered setting enclosed by steep cliffs with greenery, a small chapel and fishing boats. Well equipped, with tavernas and all water sports plus a waterslide, paragliding, scuba-diving.

ORNOS 2.5 km south of Mykonos Town.
Frequent buses from Mykonos Town.
*Long, coarse-sand beach set in a large, sheltered bay with the picturesque backdrop of a windmill, a church and a dovecote (see **A-Z**). Popular with families. Facilities include tavernas and restaurants; sunshades; volleyball; scuba-diving, windsurfing and pedaloes.*

AGHIOS STEFANOS 3 km north of Mykonos Town.
Frequent buses from Mykonos Town.
Long, coarse- and fine-sand beach popular with families and package holiday-makers. There are cliffs to one side and an open bay to the other. Tavernas, bars, restaurant; sunshades; water-skiing, windsurfing.

Mykonos Town

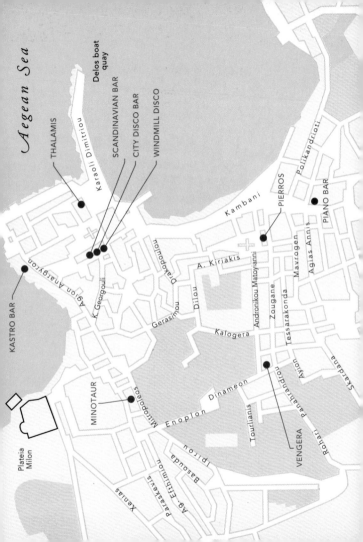

Aegean Sea

THALAMIS

Delos boat quay

Karaoli Dimitriou

SCANDINAVIAN BAR

CITY DISCO BAR

WINDMILL DISCO

KASTRO BAR

Agion Anargyron

K. Georgouli

D. Koutsou

Gerasimou

Dilou

Kalogera

A. Kiriakis

Kambani

PIERROS

Polikandrioti

PIANO BAR

Mavrogen

Agias Annis

Androuikou Matoyianni

Zougane

Tessarakonda

Plateia Milon

MINOTAUR

Mitropoleos

Enoplon

Dinameon

Ipiron

Dimitrandriou

Touplianis

VENGERA

Rohari

Skarpana

Xenias

Paraskevi

Basouda

Ag. Efthimiou

Nightlife

KASTRO BAR Agion Anargyron, Mykonos Town.
Classical music bar with splendid views to the windmills. Traditional dark-wood, white-wall interior. Popular with gay crowd. Good cocktails.

PIANO BAR Plateia Manto Mavrogenous, Mykonos Town.
A pleasant bar with live piano music. Small balcony bar overlooks the harbour. Comfy seating, relaxed atmosphere and extensive cocktail list.

MINOTAUR Mitropoleos, Mykonos Town.
Small, attractive, relaxed cocktail bar, perfect for a drink and a coffee at the end of the evening. Friendly service.

PIERROS Andronikou Matoyianni, Mykonos Town.
Lively meeting place patronized by the gay fraternity. Large, seated, terrace area and indoor bar which becomes a candlelit disco-dancing floor.

WINDMILL DISCO K. Georgouli, Mykonos Town.
A good, basic disco with small dance floor around a palm tree and a mini-windmill. Lively, easy-going atmosphere. Cheap drinks.

CITY DISCO BAR K. Georgouli, Mykonos Town.
This popular disco has the best drag show in town, on every night at 0100. Admission is 800 Drs at weekends, redeemable against first drink.

SCANDINAVIAN BAR K. Georgouli, Mykonos Town.
The liveliest meeting place in town, attracting a mixed crowd, with two bars, a large patio, a packed disco and cheap drinks.

VENGERA Enoplon Dinameon, Mykonos Town.
Smart two-storey 'colonial interior' cocktail bar and disco with small, tree-shaded patio. Gay waiters and customers.

THALAMIS Karaoli Dimitriou, Mykonos Town.
Small cellar bar playing lively, loud Greek music which entices locals and holidaying Greeks to put on impromptu floor shows of high-spirited dancing and glass-balancing. Authentic atmosphere. Cheap drinks.

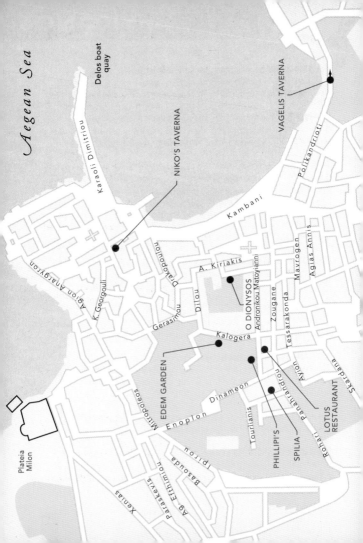

Aegean Sea

Delos boat
quay

Karaoli Dimitriou

NIKO'S TAVERNA

VAGELIS TAVERNA

Polikandrioti

Kambani

K. Georgouli

Agion Anargyron

A. Kiriakis

Drakopoulou

Dilou

Gerasimou

O DIONYSOS

Androníkou Matoyianni

Zougane

Mavrogen

Agias Annis

Tessarakonda

Kalogera

EDEM GARDEN

Enopion

Mitropoleos

Dinameon

Avlon

Panachrandrou

Rohari

LOTUS
RESTAURANT

Skardana

Tourlianis

PHILLIPI'S

SPILIA

Ipirou

Basoula

Ag. Efthimiou

Paraskevis

Xenas

Plateia
Milon

EDEM GARDEN Kalogera, Mykonos Town.
❑ Expensive.
*Large, romantic, garden restaurant with cactus, vines and bougainvillea. International/Greek menu with good lamb specials (see **Food**). Top quality, large portions and efficient service.*

PHILLIPI'S Off Enoplon Dinameon, Mykonos Town.
❑ Expensive.
The most attractive garden restaurant on Mykonos, with a dining terrace above its sunken garden. Limited menu, with mostly international dishes.

NIKO'S TAVERNA Off K. Georgouli, Mykonos Town.
❑ Moderate.
*Popular, lively taverna with jolly gingham tablecloths, a brightly painted, barrel-lined dining room and interesting Greek menu (see **Food**).*

LOTUS RESTAURANT Andronikou Matoyianni, Mykonos Town.
❑ Moderate.
*Romantic little bougainvillea-decked terrace and bar lead to a tiny dining room in an old house. Small but interesting Greek/international menu (see **Food**).*

O DIONYSOS Off Andronikou Matoyianni, Mykonos Town.
❑ Moderate.
*Large, vine-covered, statue-populated garden restaurant. Mostly Greek (see **Food**), with some international dishes. Good meats from the spit.*

SPILIA Fil Etairias, Mykonos Town.
❑ Inexpensive.
*Small, quiet, 'hole-in-the-wall' basic taverna, tucked away from the mainstream bustle. Some Mykonian specialities on offer (see **Food**).*

VAGELIS TAVERNA Houlakia, 6 km north of Mykonos Town.
❑ Inexpensive.
Excellent traditional home-made food served in basic surroundings by 'charismatic' chef/owner. Limited menu.

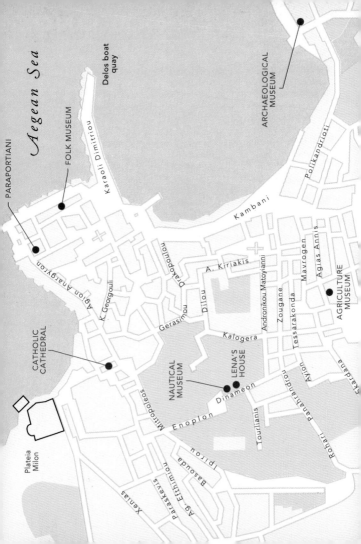

Aegean Sea

PARAPORTIANI

FOLK MUSEUM

Delos boat quay

ARCHAEOLOGICAL MUSEUM

Karaoli Dimitriou

Polikandrioti

Kambani

Agion Anargyron

Drakopoulou

A. Kiriakis

Andronikou Matoyianni

Mavrogen

Agias Annis

K. Georgouli

Gerasimou

Dilou

Zougane

Tessarakonda

AGRICULTURE MUSEUM

CATHOLIC CATHEDRAL

Katogera

Enoplon

NAUTICAL MUSEUM

LENA'S HOUSE

Dinameon

Tourlianis

Panahrandou

Aylon

Rohari

Skarpana

Mitropoleos

Plateia Milon

Basouda

Ipiron

Ag. Efthimiou

Paraskevas

Xenias

What to See

FOLK MUSEUM Near Delos boat quay, Mykonos Town.
❏ 1730-2030 Mon.-Sat.,1830-2030 Sun. ❏ Free.
Splendid collection of 19thC Mykonian art and artefacts in a period mansion. Features a reconstructed bedroom, kitchen and drawing room.

PARAPORTIANI Off Agion Anargyron, Mykonos Town.
The most photographed church in Greece, this is actually five chapels moulded into one. The heart of the small 'sugar-iced' complex dates from the 16th-17thC. Seldom open, but its beauty lies without.

CATHOLIC CATHEDRAL Between Mitropoleos and the sea, Mykonos Town.
The most beautiful church interior in Mykonos, covered entirely in bright murals (see **Customs***). The exterior is medieval, its doorway inscribed with the coat of arms of the Ghisis, rulers of Mykonos from 1207-1390.*

NAUTICAL MUSEUM OF THE AEGEAN
Tria Pigadia, Mykonos Town. ❏ 1100-1300, 1800-2100. ❏ 100 Drs.
Excellent, well laid-out displays on Aegean shipping history, featuring lovely old model ships and many interesting relics. Beautiful garden with working 19thC lighthouse lantern.

LENA'S HOUSE Tria Pigadia, Mykonos Town.
❏ 1900-2100. ❏ Free.
Ground floor of early 19thC middle-class Mykonian residence in a complete state of preservation. Fine prints, tapestries and rich furnishings.

AGRICULTURE MUSEUM Ano Mili, Mykonos Town.
A small complex of buildings with displays of local agricultural history. The 16thC Bonis windmill is renovated to working order.

ARCHAEOLOGICAL MUSEUM Ag. Stefanos road, Mykonos Town.
❏ 0830-1500 Tue.-Sat., 0900-1400 Sun. & hol. ❏ 200 Drs.
Five rooms and a courtyard displaying pottery and storage jars dating back to the 3rd millenium BC. Has a rich collection of funerary ceramics from Rheneia (Greater Delos; see **Delos***) and rare Trojan War reliefs.*

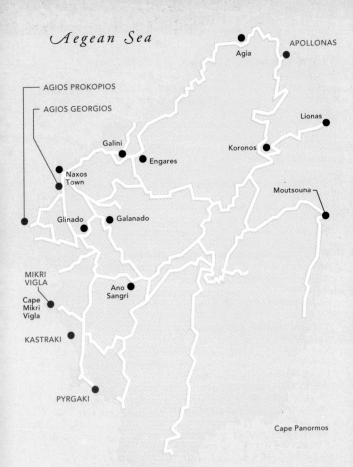

AGIOS GEORGIOS Naxos Town.
5 min walk from the port.
The main beach is half a km of compacted sand set in a calm, shallow bay. Popular with families and children, it tends to get very crowded. Further round the bay the beach is duned and wilder. All water sports, plus dinghy-sailing, are available.

AGIOS PROKOPIOS South of Naxos Town, 12 km by major road
to Agia Anna, 5 km by minor road.
From the port: 1 hr 15 min walk, hourly bus and caïque (boat).
Beautiful, white, coarse-sand beach stretching some half a km round a gently curving bay. Excellent swimming. A taverna provides the only shade. Windsurfing and jet-bikes.

MIKRI VIGLA 16 km south of Naxos Town.
Bus from Naxos Town then 15 min walk.
Two long, coarse-sand beaches, the larger to the south of Cape Mikri Vigla. The smaller north beach, backed by a holiday development, is good for windsurfing. Both beaches have tavernas.

KASTRAKI 18 km south of Naxos Town.
Bus from Naxos Town then 10 min walk.
Large, open bay with some 2 km of fine, gently shelving sand, plus a series of lovely small bays. A few juniper trees and two tavernas provide the only shade.

PYRGAKI 21 km south of Naxos Town.
Bus from Naxos Town.
A series of three small bays backed by dunes and trees. The furthest is a lovely, wide stretch of fine, golden sand, well sheltered by a cliff. Little shade other than in the tavernas. Water-skiing.

APOLLONAS North of Naxos Town, 54 km by main roads, 30 km
by minor roads. Coach excursions or public bus from Naxos Town.
Beautiful, small, sandy beach, usually host to coach parties. Lively little resort with tavernas, bars and restaurants. See NAXOS-EXCURSION.

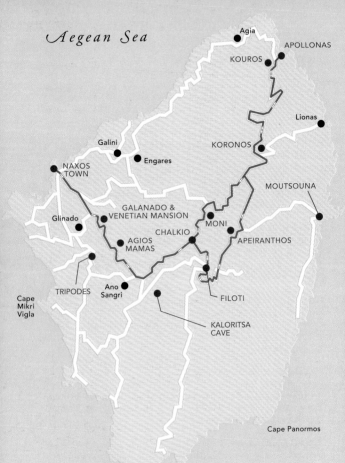

Aegean Sea

Agia
APOLLONAS
KOUROS
Lionas
Galini
Engares
KORONOS
NAXOS TOWN
MOUTSOUNA
GALANADO & VENETIAN MANSION
Glinado
MONI
CHALKIO
AGIOS MAMAS
APEIRANTHOS
TRIPODES
Ano Sangri
FILOTI
Cape Mikri Vigla
KALORITSA CAVE
Cape Panormos

Excursion

*A one-day excursion from Naxos Town (see **Naxos**) through the interior and to the north through spectacular mountain scenery to the seaside village of Apollonas. (You may also consider taking an organized coach tour which will omit the Kaloritsa cave but include all other attractions. This will be far less tiring than driving, and museums and churches are guaranteed to be open when you arrive.)*

Head out of Naxos Town past the Kastro (castle) and across the fertile Livadi plain towards Galanado.

7 km – The Bellonia Venetian Mansion. This ancient fortification looms above Galanado (see **Venetians**). Away to the south are the three windmills of Tripodes and back towards Naxos Town is a splendid view of the Livadi plain.

8 km – Agios Mamas. This ancient church, dating back to the 9thC, was once the main church of Naxos (see **Customs**). From here on there are spectacular mountain views.

12 km – The Kaloritsa Cave. About 1 km from the main road. It contains three small churches boasting unique Byzantine murals.

16 km – Chalkio. A typical small village with an excellent church, Our Lady Protothronos, and a pleasant square with a basic *kafenion* (café) and an interesting traditional shoe shop. Just off the square is the Gratsias Mansion, built to house Venetian tax-collecting officials. The marks running down the walls are said to have been made by boiling oil, used to repel attackers.

19 km – Filoti. A large, bustling village with a fine church, Our Lady Filotissa. High on a peak opposite is the splendidly isolated church of Agios Ioannis to which the villagers make an annual pilgrimage. From here to Apeiranthos, the views are stunning.

27 km – Apeiranthos (Apirathos). The entrance to this attractive marble-paved village is dominated by the Venetian Zevgolis Mansion. There are two small museums here: an excellent folklore collection which includes Naxiote bagpipes, and an archaeological museum. After leaving Apeiranthos look down to the right to Moutsouna. Now a small beach resort, it was once the export harbour for the emery industry (unique to Naxos) and the cable cars and pylons used to transport the emery are still visible there, frozen in time.

36 km – Koronos. A small, pretty, hillside village.

53 km – The Kouros of Apollonas. A huge, 10-m-long statue (see **Kouros**) of Dionysus, the god of wine and bounty, which was abandoned here where it was being carved in the 6thC, possibly because the marble was too badly cracked to continue. It was probably destined for Delos (see **DELOS-EXCURSION**, **A-Z**).

54 km – Apollonas. A lovely, picturesque fishing village-turned-holiday resort (see **NAXOS-BEACHES**).

Return to Koronos and after 2 km turn right to Moni.

80 km – Moni, Church of Our Lady Drosiani. This ancient, atmospheric church is claimed to be the oldest and one of the most important in the Balkans. The oldest part, with frescoes of saints and Jesus, dates from the 4th-5thC and the whitewashed part is anywhere between 600 and 1000 years old.

Continue for 3 km to Chalkio and return to Naxos Town. The total round trip is 96 km.

Our Lady Drosiani

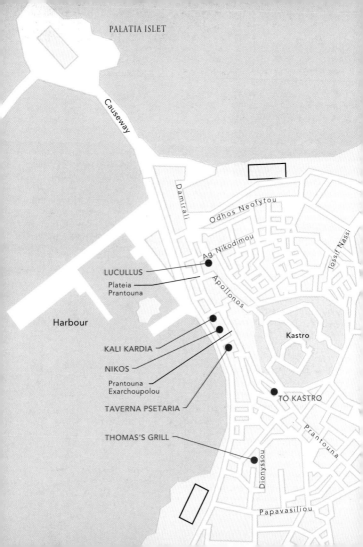

PALATIA ISLET

Causeway

Harbour

Damirali

Odhos Neofytou

Ag. Nikodimou

Apollonos

Iossif Nassi

Kastro

LUCULLUS

Plateia
Prantouna

KALI KARDIA

NIKOS

Prantouna
Exarchoupolou

TAVERNA PSETARIA

TO KASTRO

Prantouna

THOMAS'S GRILL

Dionyssou

Papavasiliou

Restaurants

NIKOS Naxos Town waterfront. Entrance on Prantouna Exarchoupolou.
❏ Expensive.
Eat indoors with a view over the harbour or outside on the pleasant rear terrace where a flaming barbecue and an impressive display of crustaceans and huge groupers attract passers-by.

TO KASTRO Prantouna, Naxos Town.
❏ Moderate.
In a lovely setting at the foot of the Kastro (castle), with tables clustered round a statue on a dimly lit patio. Nice atmosphere and good-quality food with interesting oven-beef specialities. Good service.

THOMAS'S GRILL Dionyssou, Naxos Town.
❏ Moderate.
*Basic restaurant set in a cul-de-sac with a pleasant, tree-shaded terrace. The menu is only in Greek and service is slow but the souvlakia and chips (their speciality) is worth the wait (see **Food**).*

LUCULLUS Agios Nikodimou, Naxos Town.
❏ Moderate.
*Reputedly the oldest traditional taverna in Naxos (est. 1908). Picture-postcard interior with whitewashed walls, blue doors and Naxiote bric-a-brac. Outside is a romantically lit alleyway. Good traditional food (see **A-Z**) with large portions but erratic service.*

TAVERNA PSETARIA Naxos Town waterfront.
❏ Inexpensive.
Small, basic taverna sporting a blue-and-white colour scheme, with tables on either side of the road on the seafront. Clean, friendly and family-run, with home-produced meat. Wonderful spinach pie!

KALI KARDIA Naxos Town waterfront.
❏ Inexpensive.
Busy, basic taverna with tables on both sides of the road serving a good choice of traditional dishes at the lowest price on the waterfront. Very popular with the locals.

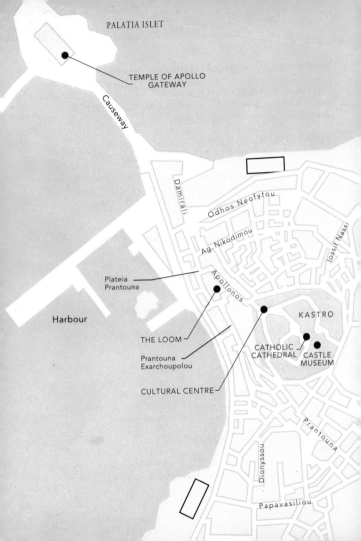

PALATIA ISLET

TEMPLE OF APOLLO
GATEWAY

Causeway

Damirali

Odhos Neofytou

Ag. Nikodimou

Iossif Nassi

Plateia
Prantouna

Apollonos

Harbour

THE LOOM

KASTRO

CATHOLIC
CATHEDRAL

CASTLE
MUSEUM

Prantouna
Exarchoupolou

CULTURAL CENTRE

Prantouna

Dionyssou

Papavasiliou

What to See

TEMPLE OF APOLLO GATEWAY Naxos Town.
*Huge portal of a temple of Apollo, god of light and music, built around 530 BC, standing on a small islet in front of the harbour. An easy climb gives good views of the Chora (see **A-Z**) on both sides of the coast.*

KASTRO (grounds only), Naxos Town.
❑ Permanently open. ❑ Free.
*The grounds of the Kastro (castle; see **Chora**) built in 1207 by Marco Sanudo (one of the first Venetians to come to the Cyclades) are entered through the original wooden door. The Crispi or Glezo tower, formerly the palace of the Venetian Dukes of Naxos, is the solitary surviving tower. See also Sanudo's Palace (not open). See **Venetians**.*

CASTLE MUSEUM (ARCHAEOLOGICAL MUSEUM)
Kastro grounds, Naxos Town.
❑ 0830-1500 Tue.-Sun. ❑ 200 Drs.
Houses an interesting large collection, including a well-preserved 4thC Roman mosaic and the famous, strangely modern-looking Cycladic idols – enigmatic marble statuettes from the 3rd millenium BC.

CATHOLIC CATHEDRAL Kastro grounds, Naxos Town.
❑ 0930 Sun. Mass.
*Built largely in the 16thC. The marble facade is a startling new addition. The floor is paved with 17th and 18thC tombstones and the 17thC sanctuary features rich baroque work (see **Customs**).*

CULTURAL CENTRE Signposted in Kastro, Naxos Town.
❑ 1100-1300, 1800-2000 Tue.-Sun. ❑ Free.
Temporary exhibitions of the works of local and other Greek artists are held in this small hall.

THE LOOM Off Apollonos, Naxos Town.
❑ Normal shop hours.
More like a tiny folk museum than a shop, the Loom sells goods ranging from local antiques and traditional costumes to old jewellery and watches, and even Naxiote bagpipes.

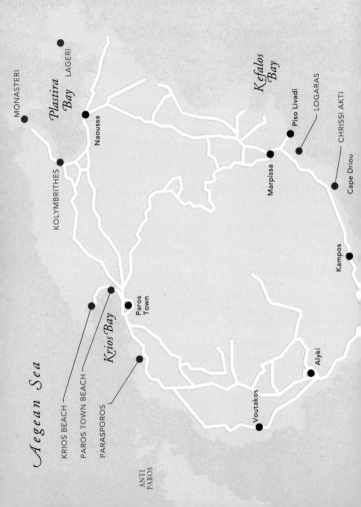

Aegean Sea

MONASTERI

Plastira Bay

LAGERI

Kefalos Bay

LOGARAS

Piso Livadi

CHRISSI AKTI

KOLYMBRITHES

Naoussa

Marpissa

Cape Driou

Kampos

Krios Bay

Paros Town

KRIOS BEACH

PAROS TOWN BEACH

PARASPOROS

Alyki

Voutakos

ANTI PAROS

KRIOS BEACH 3 km north of Paros Town.
Frequent water taxis from the port, or 30 min walk.
Small, sandy coves plus a half-km-long main beach backed by dunes.
Good swimming and snorkelling. The trendy Krios Beach Bar provides a
handy water-taxi jetty (see **Taxis**).

PAROS TOWN (LIVADIA) BEACH 0.5 km from the port.
Long, narrow beach of fine pebbly, golden sand stretching round the
bay. Scruffy in places. Trees provide shade; there are bars and tavernas.

PARASPOROS 2.5 km south of Paros Town.
Long, tree-lined, sandy beach popular with campers and nudists. It has
good swimming and all water sports.

CHRISSI AKTI (Golden Beach) 23 km southeast of Paros Town.
Frequent buses from Paros Town.
1 km of beautiful, soft, golden-duned sand, backed by bamboo. Tavernas,
bars and restaurants. A favourite spot for experienced windsurfers.

LOGARAS 0.5 km south of Piso Livadi.
Lovely half-km sweep of coarse sand with tamarisk trees for afternoon
shade. Tavernas and a café. Pedaloes and occasional windsurfing.

KOLYMBRITHES 3 km west of Naoussa port. 15 min by water taxi.
Popular spot with a small sandy beach and tiny coves in strangely weather-
shapen granite outcrops. Several tavernas. Pedaloes; good swimming.

MONASTERI 5 km north of Naoussa port. 15-20 min by water taxi.
Small, fine-sand beach with one basic taverna. The tiny sandy coves
nestling amongst the huge granite slabs are soon occupied. Canoes and
pedaloes; occasional windsurfing.

LAGERI 6 km east of Naoussa port. 25 min by water taxi.
One long, narrow, sandy beach plus one short strip of sand, set in a
well-protected bay backed by scrub, hills and fields. No tavernas but in
the high season refreshments are sold from a boat.

Aegean Sea

Plastira Bay

Kefalos Bay

Naoussa

PISO LIVADI

Logaras

CHRISSI AKTI

MARATHI QUARRIES

Marpissa

Cape Driou

LEFKES

DRIOS

Kampos

Krios Bay

PAROS TOWN

PETALOUDES

SOTIRES

ALYKI

Voutakos

ANTI PAROS

Excursion

A leisurely one-day tour of the south of the island visiting some of its beaches, the atmospheric village of Lefkes and the ancient marble quarries of Paros (see A-Z).

Head south from Paros Town, taking the coast road signposted to Pounta and Alyki. After 4 km take the left fork to Sotires. As you climb the hill, there are good views of Anti Paros (see **A-Z**) to your right. Shortly after passing through Sotires turn left.

5 km – Petaloudes. This small, wooded valley has palms, fruit trees and an ever-present stream to attract its famous *petaloudes* (butterflies). Admission is from 0900-2000, summer only, and costs 80 Drs. After your visit, backtrack to the main road.

16 km – Alyki. A pleasant little fishing port with a tree-lined beach, tavernas and a restaurant. From here until Kampos (23 km) the road is a dirt track with excellent sea views. Now and then, secluded sandy beaches, accessible only on foot, may be spotted.

29 km – Drios. Turn right off the main road by the Lake Bar sign to get to the centre of this small fishing village-cum-resort. A taverna sits on the promenade road above a shingle beach.

Lefkes

Agia Triada, Lefkes

31 km – Chrissi Akti (Golden Beach). One of the island's best beaches (see **PAROS-BEACHES**).

36 km – Piso Livadi. Small, pretty fishing village in the throes of holiday development with restaurants, tavernas and gift shops around a pleasant coarse-sand beach. Across the bay is Logaras (see **PAROS-BEACHES**). Follow the main road back inland.

43 km – Lefkes. No vehicles are allowed into this beautiful mountain village, so park in the small square near the Hotel Xenia and enjoy the views across the valley. Wander round the lovely narrow streets of crumbling buildings and eventually you will come to the village square with its basic *kafenion* (café) and tiny folk museum (1000-1400, 1700-2100. 50 Drs). Near the square is the church of Agia Triada (Holy Trinity), built in 1830 – don't miss its splendid ceiling (see **Customs**).

48 km – Marathi Quarries. Turn left immediately before a narrow bridge and a dirt track leads to the deserted quarries. Famous throughout the ancient world for the quality of their translucent marble (see **PAROS-WHAT TO SEE**), these quarries produced the stone for such works as the *Venus de Milo*, the Acropolis in Athens and the Temple of Solomon in Jerusalem. The three main shafts are still open and if you descend with care some 6 m to the entrance of the main middle shaft you will see on the left of the tunnel approach a carved relief (now in poor condition) dating from the 4thC BC. The shaft descends some 100 m but an experienced guide is recommended for further exploration (ask at the tourist information office in Paros Town – see **Paros**). The ruined buildings by the shafts are reminders of the last futile attempt to revive the shafts in 1844, although the lid of Napoleon's tomb is said to be the quarries' final great memorial.

Return on the main road back to Paros Town.

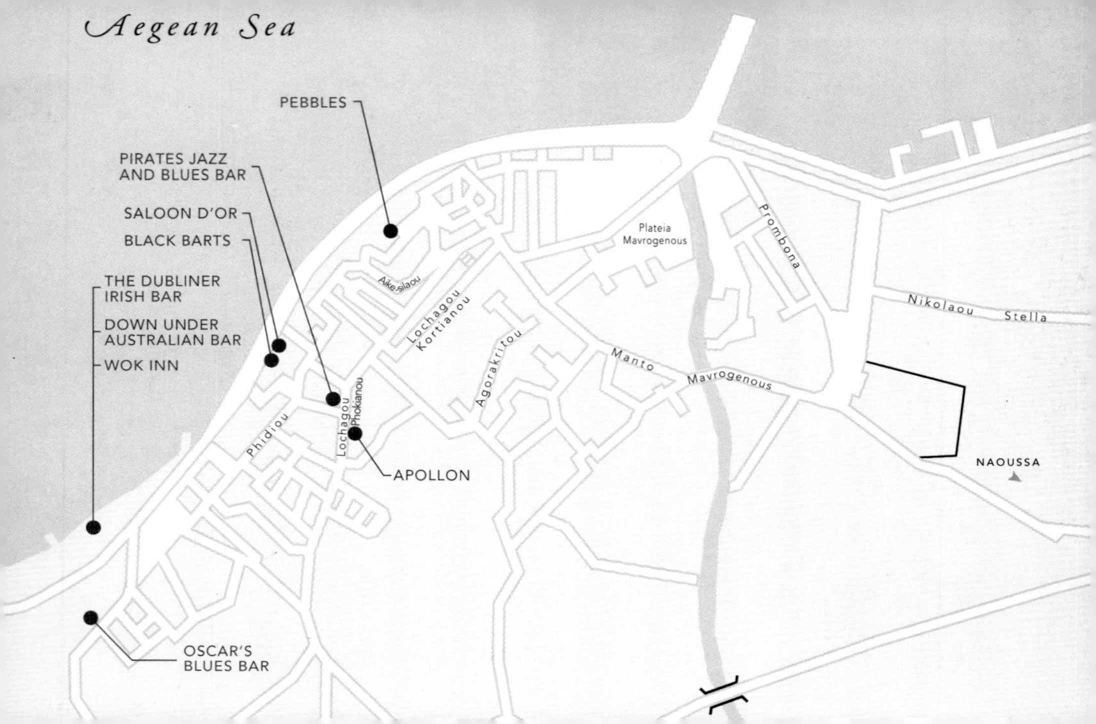

Aegean Sea

NAOUSSA

Nikolaou Stella

Promhona

Mavrogenous

Plateia
Mavrogenous

Manto

Agorakritou

Lochagou
Korrianou

Akteou

PEBBLES

APOLLON

Lochagou
Pholeanou

Phidiou

PIRATES JAZZ
AND BLUES BAR

SALOON D'OR

BLACK BARTS

THE DUBLINER
IRISH BAR

DOWN UNDER
AUSTRALIAN BAR

WOK INN

OSCAR'S
BLUES BAR

Nightlife

PEBBLES By the beach, Paros Town.
Cocktail bar playing classical and jazz music with occasional live performances. Canvas directors' chairs are set on a pleasant, open-air terrace above the sea.

PIRATES JAZZ AND BLUES BAR Off Lochagou Phokianou, Paros Town.
A music bar set in two rooms of a small, cosy, rustic house. Clientele is of a mixed age group and there is a crowded, relaxed atmosphere, with jazz and blues music.

APOLLON Off Lochagou Phokianou, Paros Town.
Cocktail bar in a beautiful, candlelit courtyard garden with a rustic trellis, palm tree and whitewashed stable block. Greek classical music and soft seats, with good cocktails and snacks.

OSCAR'S BLUES BAR By the waterfront, Paros Town.
A lively music bar offering 'German beer, English cider and cocktails'. Small and crowded, and pumping out slightly less decibels than its waterfront-bar rivals. No dancing.

SALOON D'OR/BLACK BARTS Plateia B. Argyropolou, Paros Town.
The names say it all: two loud, brash, adjacent waterfront disco-bars with lots of tables on their front terrace. These are popular youngsters' meeting places where cheap drinks are sold and consumed in copious amounts.

THE DUBLINER IRISH BAR/DOWN UNDER AUSTRALIAN BAR/WOK INN Near the windmill, Paros Town.
A popular, rowdy, mind-boggling combination of bars, discos and a Chinese restaurant, all in one large, open-air complex.

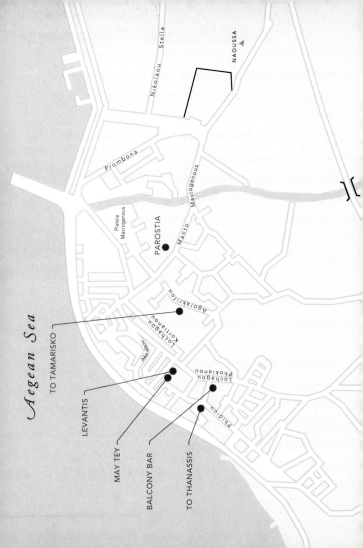

Restaurants

BALCONY BAR Off Lochagou Phokianou, Paros Town.
❏ Expensive.
Creperie/bistro with tables set on a large, attractive balcony. The classy, colonial-style interior has potted plants and a wooden floor and ceiling. 1940s/50s music plays.

LEVANTIS Off Lochagou Phokianou, Paros Town.
❏ Expensive.
*Highly regarded restaurant set in an attractive, romantic courtyard. The Lebanese chef puts together a limited but alternating menu of European, Greek (see **Food**) and Lebanese dishes. Occasional Greek dancing.*

PAROSTIA Lochagou Gravari, Paros Town.
❏ Moderate.
*Bougainvillea and hibiscus plants around a central palm give this restaurant a lovely garden setting. The international/Greek menu (see **Food**) is unadventurous but highly praised.*

TO TAMARISKO Agorakritou, Paros Town.
❏ Tue.-Sun. ❏ Moderate.
A vine-covered terrace hung with basket lamps covers this romantic, popular garden restaurant. Not an extensive menu but it is reasonably priced and has good specialities. Food is hot and portions generous.

MAY TEY Off Lochagou Phokianou, Paros Town.
❏ Moderate.
Oriental food served in well-lit, tastefully decorated, cosy rooms. Limited but interesting menu which changes daily and usually includes Vietnamese dishes. Pleasant bar area.

TO THANASSIS Off the waterfront, Paros Town.
❏ Inexpensive.
*A very basic, tiny taverna, popular with the locals and serving good, traditional food (see **A-Z**). All the dishes usually arrive together! Eat at the tables out on the pavement, or inside next to the large barrels of retsina (see **Drinks**).*

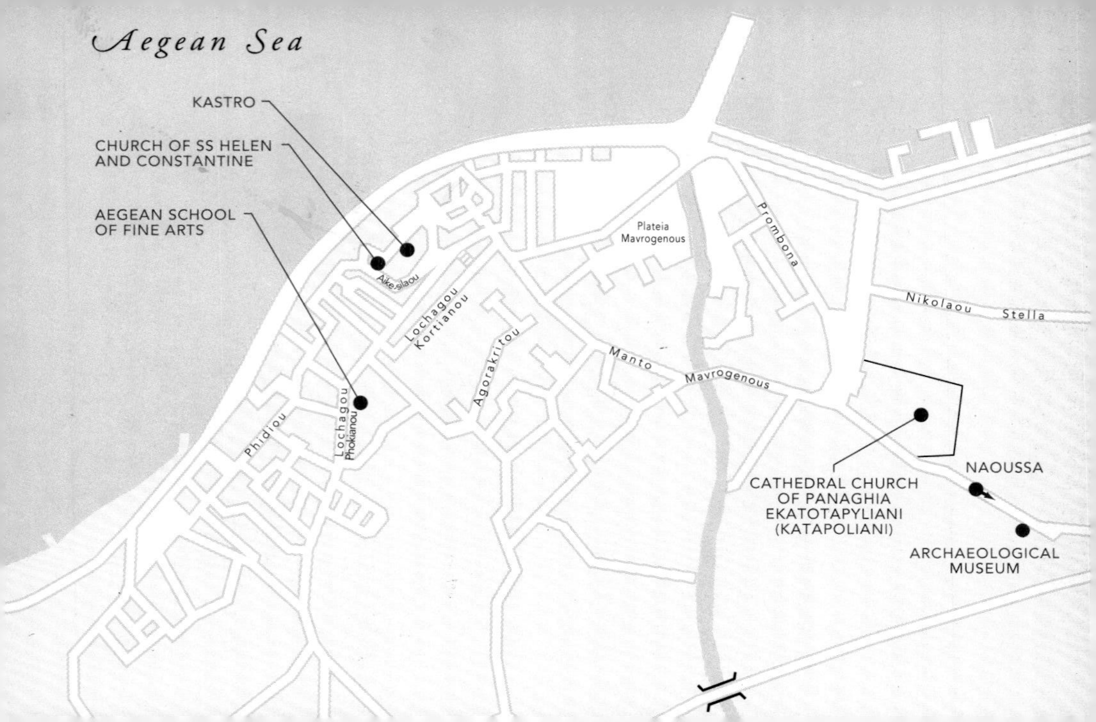

Aegean Sea

NAOUSSA

ARCHAEOLOGICAL
MUSEUM

CATHEDRAL CHURCH
OF PANAGHIA
EKATOTAPYLIANI
(KATAPOLIANI)

Nikolaou Stella

Prombona

Manto Mavrogenous

Plateia
Mavrogenous

Agorakriou

Lochagou
Korrianou

Lochagou
Ake

Lochagou
Phokianou

Phidiou

KASTRO

CHURCH OF SS HELEN
AND CONSTANTINE

AEGEAN SCHOOL
OF FINE ARTS

ARCHAEOLOGICAL MUSEUM Off Manto Mavrogenous, Paros Town.
❏ 0830-1500 Tue.-Sat., 0900-1400 Sun. & hol. ❏ 200 Drs.
*Finds from old Paroikia (see **Paros**) and the rest of the island include a piece of the famous (though unimpressive) Parian marble (see **PAROS-EXCURSION**) recording Paros life in the 4thC BC, plus a fine statue of Nike (c.500 BC), the winged goddess of victory.*

KASTRO Aikesilaou, Paros Town.
❏ Not open to the public.
*This Venetian fortress (see **A-Z**), built c.1260, is an amazing patchwork jumble of 'salvaged' materials, including large visible cross sections of columns from two temples that stood on ancient Paroikia's acropolis.*

CATHEDRAL CHURCH OF PANAGHIA EKATOTAPYLIANI (KATAPOLIANI) Off Manto Mavrogenous, Paros Town.
❏ 0800-1200, 1600-2000.
*Known as 'The Church of the Hundred Doors' (this total includes windows as well!), this is one of the oldest and most important Greek shrines, dating back to the 6thC (see **Customs**). Look out for the icons and the column carving depicting the master designer and apprentice.*

AEGEAN SCHOOL OF FINE ARTS Off Lochagou Phokianou, Paros Town.
Founded in 1966, this excellent arts centre is accredited and attended by several American universities.

CHURCH OF SS HELEN AND CONSTANTINE Paros Town.
*This lovely, colonnaded, blue-domed church overlooking the harbour dates from 1689 (see **Customs**). Beneath it, fragments of the original 7thC BC temple of Apollo, the god of light and music, can still be seen.*

NAOUSSA 11 km northeast of Paros Town. Frequent buses.
*Beautiful and largely unspoilt little fishing port and village which is much visited for its picturesque harbours, its quayside fish tavernas, several excellent beaches and its small, whitewashed Chora (see **A-Z**).*

Cable Car Ticket Office

Cable Car

M. Nomikou

Steps to port

Ag. Mina

Ipapantis

Eritrou Stavrou

STUDIO 33

25 Martiou

DIONYSUS

ENIGMA

FIRA JAZZ CLUB

TOWN CLUB

Esplanade

FRANCO'S

M. Danezi

BLUEBELL DISCO

Plateia Theotok-opoulou

FRANCO'S Esplanade by the steps to the old port, Fira.
Classy cocktail bar featuring a long terrace lined with reclining lounge chairs overlooking the bay. Live classical music nightly, with expensive drinks to match the setting.

ENIGMA Eritrou Stavrou, Fira.
Probably the most popular disco in Fira, this place enjoys a pretty, open-air setting with illuminated trees.

DIONYSUS Eritrou Stavrou, Fira.
This popular disco, with its pleasant, illuminated garden-bar and small dance floor is patronized by a slightly older crowd. Drinks are cheap earlier in the evening.

STUDIO 33 Eritrou Stavrou, Fira.
Authentic Greek dancing bar, packed with Greek holiday-makers and locals enjoying its loud Greek music, nonstop impromptu dancing, great atmosphere and cheap drinks.

TOWN CLUB Eritrou Stavrou, Fira.
This lively, noisy little one-room bar-disco, with its small dance floor, is popular with a young crowd.

FIRA JAZZ CLUB Eritrou Stavrou, Fira.
A wide range of jazz is played in the small, smoky, barrel-shaped bar-room decorated with murals. Enjoy the nice, relaxed, sleazy atmosphere. Average-priced spirits and cocktails. Popular with locals.

BLUEBELL DISCO Plateia Theotokopoulou, Fira.
A large, featureless, indoor disco which is very popular with the young crowd.

KASTRO

Cable Car Ticket Office

PETRO'S TAVERNA

Cable Car

M. Nomikou

Ipapantis

Eritrou Stavrou

25 Martiou

Steps to port

Ag. Mina

ZORBAS

NICK'S TAVERNA

Esplanade

NICKOLAOS TAVERNA

M. Danezi

NERAIDA

Plateia Theotok-opoulou

RESTAURANT BAR DOLPHIN

KASTRO Next to the cable car ticket office, Fira.
❏ Expensive.
*An attractive, top-quality, romantic restaurant which enjoys one of the best views of Fira by night. Greek/international menu (see **Food**) with steak specialities.*

ZORBAS Next to the steps to the old port, Fira.
❏ Moderate.
*Large restaurant in an attractive setting on three levels overlooking the bay. Basic Greek menu (see **Food**); some specials. Indifferent service.*

PETRO'S TAVERNA East end of N. Nomikou ('High St'), Oia.
❏ Moderate.
*Lively locals, busy, confused staff (order at the display counter) and a tatty but appealing interior combine to give bags of atmosphere. Blazing barbecue with good meats and some local specialities (see **Food**).*

NERAIDA Just off the main square, Karterados.
❏ Moderate.
Basic but popular taverna with a covered terrace. Excellent barbecued meats served by friendly staff in a lively atmosphere. Arrive early or queue.

RESTAURANT BAR DOLPHIN Perissa Beach, Perissa.
❏ Moderate.
Pleasant taverna specializing in fish and seafood, with dishes like fish plaki and octopus in a wine sauce. Service is fast and friendly.

NICK'S TAVERNA Top of the steps to the old port, Fira.
❏ Inexpensive.
Lively, cheap 'n' cheerful café/taverna catering for a noisy young crowd and with excellent views over the port. Eat early to avoid queuing.

NICKOLAOS TAVERNA Eritrou Stavrou, Fira.
❏ Inexpensive.
Small, unspoilt, 'ethnic' locals' taverna set in the narrow streets of the old town. Eating inside only.

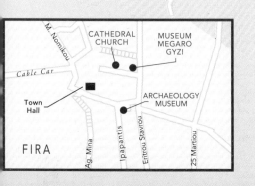

Oia

Aegean Sea

THIRASIA
ISLAND

NEA KAMENI
ISLAND

PALEA KAMENI
ISLAND

ASPRO ISLE

Firostephani

FIRA

Monolithos

Karterados

Mesaria

CANAVA
ROUSSOS

Athinos

Episkopis
Gonia

Kamari

AKROTIRI

Emporio

Perissa

M. Nomikou

CATHEDRAL
CHURCH

MUSEUM
MEGARO
GYZI

Cable Car

Town
Hall

ARCHAEOLOGY
MUSEUM

FIRA

Ag. Mina

Ipapantis

Eritrou Stavrou

25 Martiou

ARCHAEOLOGY MUSEUM Ipapantis, Fira.
❑ 0830-1500 Tue.-Sun. ❑ 200 Drs.
*Interesting, varied collection of pottery, kouroi (see **Kouros**) and relics
from Akrotiri (see below) and ancient Thera from as far back as 3000 BC.*

MUSEUM MEGARO GYZI Off Eritrou Stavrou, Fira.
❑ 1030-1330, 1700-2000. ❑ 130 Drs.
*A fine collection of engravings, maps, manuscripts, paintings and photos
of Santorini from the 16th-20thC, housed in a beautiful 18thC mansion.*

CATHEDRAL CHURCH AND DOMINICAN CONVENT
Off Eritrou Stavrou, Fira.
❑ Cathedral normally open during the day, Convent 1800-2100,
Convent church (Rosaria) open during the day, closed 1300-1600.
*The Cathedral church, built in 1823 but heavily restored, is well worth a
visit (see **Customs**). In the courtyard of the Convent church (built in
1825) there is a carpet-knotting school for local orphans.*

NEA KAMENI AND PALEA KAMENI ISLANDS
Boat trip from Fira port; book with travel agency. ❑ About 750 Drs.
*Walk around the lunar-like island of Nea Kameni, the heart of the now-
dormant volcano which last erupted in 1950 and where emissions of sul-
phur smoke may sometimes be seen. The boat will stop on the way back
for swimming in the bubbling, warm, volcanic springs off Palea Kameni.*

CANAVA ROUSSOS Near Episkopis Gonia (Mesa Gonia).
6 km south of Fira on the road to Kamari. ❑ 1400-2000. ❑ 400 Drs.
*Taste the six wines of Santorini's oldest vineyard (est. 1836, although
wine is no longer made here) and see the old wine-making equipment.*

AKROTIRI (Excavations), 14 km south of Fira.
❑ 0845-1500 Mon.-Sat., 0930-1430 Sun. & hol. ❑ 500 Drs.
*Ancient city with Minoan links, buried under volcanic ash in 1500 BC.
Ten houses (some two-storey) have so far been uncovered. All treasures
and frescoes were moved to Athens but the site is still very worthy of a
visit. A guide is essential – book in advance or take a tour from Fira.*

Ermoupolis harbour

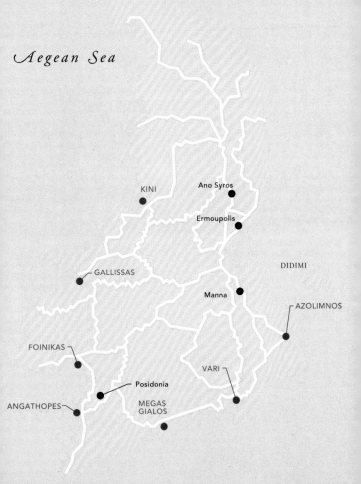

Aegean Sea

KINI

Ano Syros

Ermoupolis

GALLISSAS

DIDIMI

Manna

AZOLIMNOS

FOINIKAS

VARI

Posidonia

ANGATHOPES

MEGAS
GIALOS

Beaches

AZOLIMNOS 6 km south of Ermoupolis.
Bus from Ermoupolis to Manna then 3 km walk.
A small hamlet with a sandy beach which is popular with the locals.
Basic kafenions (cafés) provide the refreshment.

VARI 9 km south of Ermoupolis. Bus from Ermoupolis.
Small, broad, fine-sand beach set in a pretty, secluded bay protected on
both sides by tall cliffs. Tavernas and hotels. Pedaloes.

MEGAS GIALOS 14 km south of Ermoupolis. Bus from Ermoupolis.
A small, sandy cove overlooked by the church of Agias Thekla. Trees
hide the beach from the main road and offer some shade. There is a
pizza restaurant close by.

ANGATHOPES 13 km southwest of Ermoupolis.
Bus from Ermoupolis to Posidonia (Delagratsia) then 1 km walk.
Open, sandy beach stretching 100 m, backed by trees and some 'beach
cactus'. A few beach shades, one taverna and a hotel restaurant.
Windsurfing and pedaloes.

FOINIKAS 12 km southwest of Ermoupolis. Bus from Ermoupolis.
Long, narrow, tree-lined, fine-sand and pebble beach set in a large,
pleasant bay and popular with families. Hotels, restaurants and tavernas
offer shade and sustenance. Windsurfing and water-skiing.

GALLISSAS 9 km west of Ermoupolis. Bus from Ermoupolis.
Pleasant, sandy, 150-m-long crescent-shaped beach set well back in a
protected bay and backed by trees and a camping site. There are taver-
nas, restaurants and bars on the track leading to beach. Windsurfing and
pedaloes. A track beside the church leads to a small nudist beach.

KINI 9 km west of Ermoupolis. Bus from Ermoupolis.
Long, sandy beach planted with some trees and bamboo shades, and set
in the large, attractive, sheltered bay of a fishing village. Basic tavernas
provide shade and refreshment.

ANO SYROS
(by foot)

Anaxagora

D. Kontouli

Ladopoulou

VRONTADO
AGIOS
NIKOLAOS

Chalepa

Louka Ralli

I. Chalika

Filippotou

Plateia
Vardaka

Valiadaki

Karaoli & Dimitriou

TOWN HALL

Chris. Evagelidou

Apollonos

ARCHAEOLOGICAL
MUSEUM

G. Souri

Plateia Miaoulis

Leotsakou

G. Stavrou

Rousvelt

N. Papadam

Kotsovili

Stefanou

Omirou

Iroon

Protopapadaki

Evagelistrias

Parou

Antiparou

Eleftheriou Venizelou

Xiochio

Akti Ethniki   Antistasis

Eptanisou

Akti P. Ralli

Harbour

Plateia
Kanari

Asklipiou

Stam Proiou

Papadam

Plateia
Evropis

ANO SYROS (by road)
CHURCH OF THE ASSUMPTION
MONASTERY/CONVENT OF SANTA BARBARA

What to See

ANO SYROS Ermoupolis.

By foot, 800 steps adjacent to the Town Hall; by car, head 0.5 km south of the town and turn right.

*Towering above 19thC Ermoupolis is the original Chora (see **A-Z**), founded in the 14thC. A typical whitewashed maze is surmounted by the Catholic Cathedral of St. George, founded in the 17thC.*

VRONTADO Ermoupolis.

*The second hill of Ermoupolis, topped by the spectacular Greek Orthodox Church of Anastais which has some fine, ancient icons (see **Customs**). Excellent views east as far as Mykonos (see **A-Z**).*

TOWN HALL Plateia Miaoulis, Ermoupolis.

Splendid, early-19thC, neoclassical building, more north European than Greek. Not officially open, but you can look inside its galleried towers.

ARCHAEOLOGICAL MUSEUM Rear (left) of the Town Hall,
Ermoupolis. ❑ 0900-1500 Mon., Wed.-Sat., 0930-1430 Sun. & hol.
❑ 200 Drs.

*Features Cycladic and Roman finds from Syros (see **A-Z**), Paros (see **A-Z**) and Amorgos (see **A-Z**), including enigmatic Cycladic idol statuettes.*

AGIOS NIKOLAOS Ladopoulou, Ermoupolis.

*Beautiful, blue-domed Greek Orthodox church with impressive stone-carved altar screen (see **Customs**). The Unknown Warrior (1881) in front of the church is claimed to be the first of its kind in the world.*

CHURCH OF THE ASSUMPTION Stam Proiou, Ermoupolis.

Beautiful interior with many old pictures in the nave and ambulatories.

MONASTERY/CONVENT OF SANTA BARBARA
(AGIAS VARVARAS) 4 km from Kini, 5 km from Ermoupolis.

*This lovely convent, set high above Kini, welcomes visitors (see **Customs**). You will be taken into the church to see the frescoes depicting the martyrdom of the Saint, and to the small workshop where orphans produce traditional, hand-woven cloth items which are for sale.*

Accidents & Breakdowns: If you are involved in a road accident exchange names and insurance details (ensure you have the relevant information to hand if you are hiring). The police are unlikely to intervene unless someone has been injured, in which case you must contact them and then take advice from your consulate in Athens. Try to be particularly careful on motorbikes and scooters.

You won't find any breakdown services if you go exploring inland and there are few properly equipped garages even in the major settlements. Try to pre-empt problems by inspecting the vehicle before you take it out, checking tyres, water, oil and battery levels. See **Bicycle & Motorcycle Hire**, **Car Hire**, **Consulates**, **Emergency Numbers**.

Accommodation: The vast majority of accommodation is provided by private rooms and small hotels. Studios and apartments are not common and high-rise blocks non-existent. Hotels range from first-class A to fifth-class E. There are only a handful of As on the islands, most hotels being C or below. A C-class hotel will usually offer *en suite* facilities (but always ask) and the average price for an *en suite* double room in the high season is between 3000-5000 Drs per night (excluding

breakfast). All hotels are subject to tourist police regulations (see **Police**) and the room tariff should be pinned to the back of the room door. Rooms in houses or tavernas and pensions can range from very basic to good-hotel class. As a rule you will get what you pay for. The most basic rooms with shared facilities start at around 1000 Drs per night.

If you visit the more popular islands in high season without a room reservation you will almost certainly find reasonable accommodation hard to get. However, as you get off the ferry you will be swamped by room owners almost carrying you off bodily to private houses and rooms. If none of these take your fancy try the local tourist information office who will advise on availability. Most islands have organized camp sites. See **Camping**, **Tourist Information**, **Youth Hostels**.

Airport: If you are flying from Britain to the Cyclades you may well be unable, regrettably, to avoid Athens airport. The staff here can be incredibly rude and the airport seems to be in a constant state of chaos. If you have an interconnecting flight to Mykonos, Paros, Santorini or Milos double-check your arrangement on arrival, check in as early as possible and keep your fingers crossed! See **Athens**.

Amorgos: 121 sq km. The most easterly of the Cyclades, Amorgos boasts a dramatic, rugged, barren landscape. There are three main settlements: the ports of Aegiali and Katapola, and the Chora (see **A-Z**), a typical, picturesque, whitewashed capital with a ruined castle and abandoned windmills. The pace of life is slow and authentically Greek but the first signs of tourism are showing, most notably (though not in particularly good taste) at Aegiali which is blessed with the island's best beaches. The 11thC monastery of Hozoviotizza, huddled against a sheer cliff 300 m above the sea, is definitely worth a visit, as is the pleasant village of Langada.

Getting there: By ferry, Piraeus (mainland) 11-13 hr; daily boats in summer from Naxos, 3-5 hr. Direct links: Paros, Naxos, Ios, Little Cyclades.
Getting about: Moped hire; frequent bus service between Chora, Katapola and the local beach of Ag. Anna; minibus between Aegiali and Chora twice a day; few taxis.

Anafi: 38 sq km. A small, quiet, undeveloped island with a few beaches, a handful of tavernas and a monastery to visit. This is the most southerly of the inhabited Cyclades and its only concessions to tourism are a new road between its port Ag. Nikolaos and its Chora (see **A-Z**), and a couple of tourist shops.
Getting there: By ferry, Piraeus (mainland) 13-19 hr, dependent on route; regular service in summer from Santorini. Direct links: Santorini, Ios.

Andros: 379 sq km. The northernmost of the Cyclades and, after Naxos, the most mountainous island of the group. Consequently the scenery in parts is spectacular, particularly around Profit Ilias (995 m; see **ANDROS-EXCURSION**), and lush, with serried ranks of cypress trees a common sight. Surprisingly for such a large, attractive island close to Athens, tourism here is less developed than on any of the islands in the eastern chain with the exception of Syros. This does not mean that the main towns, Andros Town and Batsi, are quiet: rather, they are at the stage of having been discovered but not overrun (see **ANDROS-EXCURSION**). Batsi is an idyllic fishing harbour (albeit now with tourist bars and a couple of discos), whereas Andros Town is an elegant Chora (see **A-Z**) with two large beaches (see **ANDROS-BEACHES**). The imposing 19thC sea merchants' mansions in Andros Town are typical of the island's wealthy maritime legacy. In addition to the fine museums (see **ANDROS-EXCURSION**) in the Chora there is an impressive 20-m-high tower (of unknown provenance) at Ag. Petros (near Gavrion) and the monasteries of Zoodochou Pigia (between Chora and Batsi) and Panachrantos.

Getting there: By ferry, Rafina (mainland) 2 hr 30 min. Direct links: Tinos, Syros. Getting about: Motorbike hire; car hire; regular bus services; taxi service; water taxis to the more isolated beaches. Tourist information: Dolfin Hellas, Batsi. Day trips: Tinos, Mykonos, Delos. See **ANDROS**.

Anti Paros: 35 sq km. The perfect bolt hole when Paros (see **A-Z**) gets too busy. Anti Paros is usually treated as a day trip from its big sister but has enough to warrant a longer stay. The one and only settlement on this small, barren, peaceful island is also called Anti Paros. This is a lively place without being spoiled and has bars, restaurants and the obligatory discos. Ten minutes' walk away is a good sandy beach popular with windsurfers and nudists. There is also a handful of other beaches. The main attraction is the Cave (summer 0900-1500, 350 Drs), which is famous for its stalactites and stalagmites. This is 7 km from the town and is reached either by minibus, mule, caïque (a long, narrow, lightweight boat), or some boat trips from Paros which go there direct.

Getting there: Regular ferry service (minimum twice daily) from Paros Town (45 min) or by caïque from Pounta on Paros (10 min). Getting about: No public transport or vehicle hire. Direct links/tourist information: see **Paros**.

Antiques: It is illegal to take Greek antiques out of the country without prior permission which involves an enormous amount of paperwork. Those found guilty of illegally exporting antiques face prosecution and stiff penalties.

Athens: Unless you enjoy stress it is not a good idea simply to tag Athens on to the end of an island holiday without pre-planning and pre-booking. It is extremely noisy, busy and polluted, and it is not easy to find good-value accommodation. However, with some advance planning, the delights of the Acropolis, the splendid museums and the huge flea market are just some of its sights which are well worth a visit. Beware when taking a taxi, particularly between Athens airport and the port of Piraeus. It is not uncommon for fares of up to 20,000 Drs (around £80) to be demanded from tourists for a 45 min journey which would cost less than the equivalent of 80p on the bus. See **Complaints**.

Baby-sitters: Ask at your hotel reception or speak to your travel representative. See **Children**.

Banks: See **Currency**, **Money**, **Opening Times**.

Beaches: The Cyclades possess some of the best sandy beaches in Europe. Moreover, the Aegean is far cleaner than much of the northern Mediterranean. As a general rule, the further you go from town the more unspoilt the beach will be. This applies even to Mykonos (see **A-Z**) where, at the height of the season, near-deserted sands can still be found. See **BEACHES** by island.

Best Buys: The islanders, in general, are not devoted to extracting the tourists' drachmas and there are few obvious 'best buys' or any merchandise that is produced solely by one island. Mykonos (see **A-Z**) abounds with expensive fashion boutiques while the streets of Fira on Santorini (see **A-Z**) glitter with jewellers, but neither of these are Greek. For clothing and accessories, leather goods and sandals in particular are always good value, and all the islands sell woollen knitwear. For Graecophiles and history fans good, inexpensive copies of museum pieces – including the popular Cycladic idol statuettes – are widely available. So too are sponges, sometimes sold straight off the boat. If you want a taste of Greece buy *kitron*, a lemon liqueur (see **Drinks**) from Naxos (see **A-Z**), *loukoumi* (Turkish delight) or nougat (see **Food**) from Syros (see **A-Z**), or honey, pistachio nuts and olive oil which come from anywhere in Greece. See **Shopping**.

Bicycle & Motorcycle Hire: This is often an excellent way to get round an island, with the ability to negotiate the narrow dirt tracks that four-wheeled vehicles cannot use. Unless you are used to two-wheeled travel, however, take care. Make sure you are insured not only by the hire company (comprehensive cover may cost more than the price you are quoted, so check) but also by your personal accident insurance. Finally, check the bike out as thoroughly as possible (brakes, lights, etc.) before setting off. See **Accidents & Breakdowns**, **Driving**, **Emergency Numbers**, **Health**, **Insurance**.

Boat Services: Although much maligned on grounds of reliability –
some national tour operators cite this as a reason not to run packages to
the islands – most inter-island ferryboats do stick to the timetables. The
boats range from smallish double-deckers carrying a couple of hundred
people, to giant ocean-going liners with TV lounges, restaurants and
several different deck classes. It is worth upgrading for the sake of a few
more drachmas on a long journey. Most ports have whole rows of
quayside travel agents, many of whom are selling the same boat tickets
and who display the times and destinations of ferries on blackboards.
If in doubt consult the port police who always have an office on the
waterfront. See **Hydrofoils**, **Island-hopping**, **Tourist Information**.

Budget:
Breakfast, English (orange juice, bacon and eggs) 350 Drs
Breakfast, Continental 200 Drs
Lunch (two moussakas, one portion of chips and one 'Greek' salad –
see **Food** – between two, with two beers or Cokes) c.1500 Drs
Dinner see **Eating Out**
Tea/coffee 100 Drs
Beer/Coke 100 Drs
Bottle of wine in a restaurant 500-800 Drs
Sunbed hire 250-400 Drs per day
Canoes 300 Drs per hour
Pedaloes 500 Drs per hour
Windsurfing 800-1200 Drs per hour
Water-ski/jet-ski 1500-2000 Drs per 15 min
Ferry ticket, e.g. Mykonos-Paros 622 Drs
Bus ticket, e.g. 5 km journey 90 Drs
Car hire 6000-8000 Drs per day
Moped/small motorbike hire 1400-1800 Drs per day
Scooter hire 1700-2500 Drs per day

Buses: Most islands provide at least a rudimentary service and on the
more popular islands buses run every 30 min or so between the main
settlements and beaches. The majority of vehicles are pretty ancient,
but most go on time (as long as a time is stated!), while others may wait
to fill up. The bus companies' unwritten rule is to get as many people
on as possible, sometimes to an alarming degree, so it is best to arrive
early to get a seat. Fares are very cheap, a typical 5 km journey costing
around 90 Drs.

Cameras & Photography: You can buy major brands of film on
most islands and the more popular islands offer rapid-developing
services, but prices are more expensive than at home. You can take
photographs in museums (when it is allowed) and at archaeological
sites for free when using a small portable camera without a flash, but if
you use a tripod you will be charged around 1500 Drs. Don't photo-
graph anything that looks even remotely like a military installation

(including airfields), although signs will probably warn you, anyway. The Greeks have been known to jail tourists for such an offence.

Camping: The following islands have organized camp sites: Mykonos (Paradise Beach – see **MYKONOS-BEACHES 2**); Naxos (three beach sites south of Naxos Town – see **NAXOS-BEACHES**); Paros (Livadia Beach, Paros Town; Naoussa; Parasporos – see **PAROS-BEACHES**); Ios (Gialos; two sites at Milopotamos beach – see **IOS-BEACHES**); Anti Paros (see **A-Z**); Syros (Gallissas – see **SYROS-BEACHES**); Folegandros (2 km from Karavostassis; see **Folegandros**); Amorgos (near Katapola and near Aegiali, the latter very basic; see **Amorgos**); Tinos (Tinos Town; see **Tinos**); Andros (2 km from Gavrion; see **Andros**); Sifnos (Plati Gialos; see **Sifnos**); and Santorini (Perissa). The average cost per night is around 300 Drs per person plus 150 Drs per tent. Standards vary quite widely. Camping on unauthorized sites is forbidden but a blind eye is often turned, particularly if the offender is away from a main resort. Beware sites which are located close to lagoons where mosquitoes lurk.

Car Hire: This is expensive, starting from around 6000 Drs per day for a small two-door saloon (this includes local taxes but may only provide third-party insurance), rising to around 8000 Drs for a beach buggy in the high season in the more popular resorts. Comprehensive insurance cover will add around 1000 Drs per day. Weigh up the cost of hiring against the cost and ease of using public transport and taxis. Car hire is definitely worth considering on Paros (see **A-Z**), Naxos (see **A-Z**) and Andros (see **A-Z**) where the islands are quite big and there are many places off the beaten track worth seeing. You will need your driving licence and sometimes also your passport. Some firms may require drivers to be of a minimum age (21/23/25) but there are no firm rules on this. Hire directly from a hire firm if possible, as going through an agent can be more expensive, and always shop around. When hiring, do check that a day's hire means 24 hours. Finally, be careful if you hire a Suzuki jeep: Consumer Association tests show that some models may be unstable while cornering if driven too fast. See **Accidents & Breakdowns**, **Driving**, **Emergency Numbers**, **Health**, **Insurance**.

Chemists: Known as *pharmakia*, they are identifiable by a red cross on a white background. A rota system ensures there is (usually) always one chemist open or contactable at any time, day or night. Even the tiny, remote islands have their own facilities. See **Health**.

Children: The Greeks love children. They are welcome at tavernas and most of the beaches are ideal for a family holiday. However, think twice about taking young children to the islands. Few hotels below B grade are geared to children (e.g. no baby-sitting facilities), few resorts have children's amusements and the laid-back Greek service can become extremely wearing with impatient youngsters in tow. See **Baby-sitters**.

Chora: A term, literally meaning 'the place', applied to the main settlement on an island. Typically this is set a little way inland, around a hill, with a castle (*kastro*) at its heart. The siting and fortification is a historical legacy of past sufferings visited upon the islanders by pirates and raiding Turks.

Churches: Everywhere you go in the Cyclades, you will see churches. Many of these are tiny and were never meant for anything other than private family worship. In the countryside they are often an integral part of the farm, thus sparing the farmer the time spent going to the village for his daily prayers. The private church was also considered necessary in the old days, as the dead were not to be taken away from their homes. Finally, many churches were built by sailors as pledges of gratitude for having been saved at sea. See **Customs**, **Monasteries**, **Religion**.

Cinemas: Many of the larger islands boast open-air cinemas which show recent American and British releases. Admission is cheap and on summer evenings this is a pleasant and novel way to spend a couple of hours.

Climate: The average daily temperatures for the summer months in the Cyclades are as follows: May 20°C; June 23°C; July 25°C; August 25°C; September 23°C. It rains, on average, on one day per month from mid-May through to mid-September (though rarely for long), and cloudless days are the norm. The biggest problem is the meltemi, a northwesterly wind which sweeps over the whole Aegean Sea from mid-July to the end of August. Mykonos in particular is badly affected by the meltemi, and on the worst days it is impossible to lie on a beach without being sandblasted. The temperature drops surprisingly in the evening and if the wind – not necessarily the meltemi – is blowing, a jumper or light jacket is needed.

Complaints: In the event of a general complaint about a hotel, restaurant, travel agent, etc. that cannot be resolved on the spot, the tourist police or local police (see **Police**) will arbitrate.

Consulates: There is no representation on the islands. The nearest consulates are in Athens.
UK – 1 Ploutarchou St 106-75, Athens, tel: 01-7236211.
R. of Ireland – Vass. Constantinou 7, Athens, tel: 01-7212951.
Australia – 37 Dimitriou Soutso, Athens, tel: 01-6447303.
Canada – 4 I. Gennadiou St 115-21, Athens, tel: 01-7239511.
New Zealand – 15-17 An. Tsoha St 115-21, Athens, tel: 01-6410311.
USA – 91 Vass. Sofias Ave 115-21, Athens, tel: 01-7212951.

Conversion Chart:

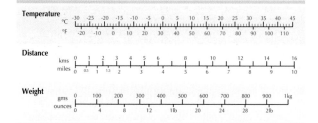

Credit Cards: See **Money**.

Crime & Theft : Greeks are, on the whole, very honest people. However, as your fellow travellers may not be so worthy, the general rules of caution apply. With the possible exception of Ios where drunken British and Italian youths can be a problem in the high season, all the Cyclades are perfectly safe, anytime of the day or night. If you are the victim of a theft, contact the police and, if necessary, your own consulate. Remember to keep a copy of the police report for any insurance claim you may make. If you are arrested for any reason, get in touch with your consulate immediately – they are obliged to find you an English-speaking lawyer. See **Consulates**, **Emergency Numbers**, **Insurance**, **Police**.

Currency: The unit of currency is the drachma. There are 1, 2, 5, 10, 20 and 50 drachmae (Drs) coins and 50, 100, 500, 1000 and 5000 Drs notes. You are not allowed to take into Greece more than 100,000 Drs or to take out more than 20,000 Drs. See **Money.**

Customs: You must be well covered up when visiting local churches and monasteries – you won't be allowed in wearing shorts or short skirts.

Customs Allowances:

Duty Paid Into:	Cigarettes	or	Cigars	or	Tobacco	Spirits	Wine
E C	300		75		400 g	1.5 *l*	5 *l*
U K	300		75		400 g	1.5 *l*	5 *l*

Delos: 3 sq km. According to the Ionians, who inhabited Delos around 1000 BC, the island was the birthplace of Apollo, god of light and music and son of Zeus (the supreme god) and Leto. During the next millenium it developed from a religious shrine into the spiritual and commercial centre of the Aegean and as the islands around it lay in a circle (for which the Greek is *kyklos*), so the name 'Kyklades' came about. Delos became the centre of the Mediterranean slave trade and on busy days up to 10,000 people would be sold here. However, due to its religious importance neither birth nor death was allowed on the island and in 540 BC and 425 BC the islands were 'cleansed' by the removal of graves, and pregnant women, to adjacent Rheneia (Greater Delos). By Roman times the island's wealthy population numbered 25,000. However, Delos was sacked by Mithridates, the King of Pontus, in 88 BC, and it never recovered. Frequently looted over the centuries, it became a haven for pirates, and much of its architecture was destroyed and its stone carried off to neighbouring Cyclades islands to be used as domestic building materials. The site was rediscovered in 1837 and this 'Greek Pompeii' has been excavated ever since. See **DELOS-EXCURSION**.

Disabled People: There are very few services for disabled travellers in the Cyclades. Olympic Airways will fly all wheelchair-users to the islands but ferry travel would be very uncomfortable, if not impossible. Roads and pavements are frequently very narrow and in poor condition, there are few public ramps, even fewer public lifts and no public wheelchair toilets. Facilities for visually handicapped people and those with hearing difficulties are equally scarce.
Notify hotels in advance if you have any special requirements and remember to read the small print on insurance documents (see **Insurance**). Also, it may not be possible to obtain certain medicines, so be sure to stock up at home before you go on holiday. See **Health**.

Discotheques: The most popular form of young nightlife on the islands. Mykonos, Paros, Santorini and Ios have the best choice, while nearly all the other islands have at least one disco. The term is often loosely applied to any loud-music bar. Few charge for entrance although a cover charge which will include your first drink may be asked at popular spots. Drink prices in discos are double or treble normal bar prices. All discos are required by law to close by 0300. See **NIGHTLIFE** by island.

Dovecotes: These are widespread on the Cyclades and nowhere more so than on Tinos (see **A-Z**). Often two storeys high, these small towers look like a cross between an elaborate chimney stack and a mini-fortress and are often decorated with geometric designs. Explanations as to the popularity of doves range from their being the descendents of the homing pigeons carried by Greek ships in pre-radio days, to the usual mythological origins. They were introduced by the Venetians (see **A-Z**) who also built many of the dovecotes.

Drinks: The Cyclades are not renowned for fine wines and with the possible exception of the produce of Paros (see **A-Z**) and Santorini (see **A-Z**) the local wine (much like the local food) is cheap and cheerful. Retsina from the barrel is the cheapest wine and should be sampled at least once (make sure it is well chilled). You'll either like or hate its strange, resinated taste. The national spirit is ouzo, an aniseed-flavoured clear drink which turns cloudy when water is added to it. This is also cheap (around 50-100 Drs per glass) and, in basic ouzerie bars or *kafenions* (cafés), may be accompanied by a small plate of *mezes* (appetizers or snacks), comprising either grilled octopus or nuts and/or sunflower seeds. *Kitron* is the lemon liqueur of Naxos (see

Best Buys). Beer is good-quality German or Dutch canned or bottled premium lager, with Amstel or Fix produced locally under licence and therefore usually slightly cheaper than other brands.

Beware of cheap cocktails, particularly on Ios but also on Paros where local 'firewater', known as *bombe* (for obvious reasons), provides the alcoholic content. This not only tastes awful, it is also mildly poisonous and dangerous if drunk in quantity.

Tea is always made from a tea bag and coffee is either a 'do-it-yourself' affair, with a sachet of instant coffee plus a pot or cup of water, or it comes milky. As Nescafé is the prevalent brand, western coffee is always referred to as 'nescafé' (*meh gala* – white, *mavro* – black). Eastern coffee or Greek coffee (don't call it Turkish, even though it is!) is a sweet, strong, black syrup including the grounds, so don't stir it and only drink just over half the tiny cup. For a less sweet version request *metrio* (supposedly medium, but still sweet) or *sketo* (no sugar). Once you taste it you'll understand why it is always served with a glass of water. A popular long, cool drink is frappé, iced coffee, western-style. A request for water (*nero*), will generally elicit a large plastic bottle of still mineral water. For a sparkling water ask for a (club) soda.

Driving: You must have an EC or international driving licence and third-party insurance to drive in Greece. Drive on the right-hand side and overtake on the left. Seat belts are now compulsory, and children are not allowed in the front seat. Due to the size of many of the islands, the poor (though navigable) road surfaces and the high cost of car hire (see **A-Z**), the Cyclades are not a motorist's paradise. Speed limits are largely irrelevant on the islands as the poor road conditions are self-regulating. However, even on good stretches of road you should drive carefully and slowly. There are no motoring organizations in the Cyclades. See **Bicycle & Motorcycle Hire**, **Car Hire**.

Drugs: The Greeks do not differentiate between hard and soft drugs and will impose strict sentences on persons carrying even small amounts of hashish. Drug trafficking can mean life imprisonment. If you are arrested for a drugs-related offence, contact your consulate (see **A-Z**).

Eating Out: The whole gastronomic spectrum of delights and disasters can be experienced in the Cyclades – from French *haute cuisine* on Mykonos to 'original fish and chips' on Ios. Of course the best-value food is Greek, be it a simple take-away souvlakia (doner-style sliced veal and salad in pitta bread) or a 'blow-out' in an authentic taverna, which could last all night and still cost less than £10 per head. Eating in a taverna is nearly always a casual and, if busy, sometimes chaotic affair. Waiters may change your order, lose your order, ignore taking your order and then finally bring all courses at once! It is always best to look at what is cooking (this is often expected anyway) as then you can see what is available and what looks fresh. The difference between a taverna and a restaurant is slight, but generally the former is family-run, less formal and often cheaper than an equivalent 'restaurant'. Lunch usually lasts from 1200-1600 and dinner from 2000-2400, but there are no rules. Price guidelines used in **RESTAURANTS**, based on a three-course meal for two with wine, are as follows, : Expensive – over 4000 Drs; Moderate – 2000-4000 Drs; Inexpensive – up to 2000 Drs. See **RESTAURANTS** by island, **Food**.

Electricity: 220 volts. Small, two-pin plugs are used. Adaptors are available in the UK and in airport shops.

Emergency Numbers:

Andros (Batsi):	Police 61216
	Clinic 61215
	Doctors 41555, 71379
	Dentist 41450
Ios (Chora):	Police 91222
	Doctor 91227
Milos (Adamas):	Police 21378
	Clinics 21222, 21218
	Doctor 22027
Mykonos (Town):	Police 22482, 22235
	Clinic 22274
	Hospital 23994
	Doctors 23026, 71395, 23888, 23946, 22530, 22130
	Dentists 22503, 23992
Naxos (Town):	Police 22100
	Clinic 22346
	Doctors 23866, 22819, 22202, 23303, 23823, 22308
	Dentists 22315, 23878, 23208, 22727, 22902
Paros (Town):	Police 21673
	Clinics 21339, 21235
Santorini (Fira):	Police 22649
	Clinics 22237, 22236
	Doctor 22820
	Dentist 22973
Sifnos (Apollonia):	Police 31210
	Clinic 31315
Syros (Ermoupolis):	Police 22610
	Hospital 22555

Most of these numbers will be answered by staff who can speak rudimentary English.

Events: Religious festivals, *panyeri*, are generally held on one of three occasions: on saints' days at those churches dedicated to the saint; on certain islands on dates of local importance; and all over the islands on dates of national religious significance. The major Greek festival time is Easter. There is always a Good Friday procession and on Easter Sunday celebrations with dancing and feasts are held in town and village squares. The other important religious date is 15 August, Assumption Day. The most popular festival on that date takes place on Tinos (see **A-Z**) but unless you are extremely interested, give it a wide berth as it becomes impossibly crowded. It is well worth trying to catch local festivities as in all probability this is the only time you will get to see real Greek dancing and singing in its natural place. In some cases you may even get to join in the celebrations but think of this as a bonus, not a right. Ask at the tourist information office (see **A-Z**) for details. See **Public Holidays**.

Folegandros: 32 sq km. One of the smallest permanently populated Greek isles, Folegandros has traditionally been a place of exile and its name means 'rocky island'. Sheer cliffs rise dramatically to over 330 m and the scenery is reminiscent of Santorini (see **A-Z**). The jewel in the

crown is the Chora (see **A-Z**), one of the most attractive in the whole of the Cyclades. There are two other main settlements, five principal beaches and the Golden Cave which is worth taking a caïque (a long, narrow, lightweight boat) out to. Tourism is just starting to arrive and overall this is one of the most rewarding of the less-developed islands. Getting there: By ferry, Piraeus (mainland) 11 hr; by air, Milos then ferry. Direct links: Milos, Sikinos, Santorini. Getting about: A regular bus service is the only form of transport. Tourist information: Chora.

Food: A typical Greek menu will include most of the following: Starters – taramasalata (pink-coloured mullet-roe dip), tzatziki (cucumber, yogurt and garlic dip), *melidzanosalata* (aubergine, onion, garlic and olive dip), *skordalia* (garlic dip, sometimes an accompaniment to battered fish), dolmades (stuffed vine leaves), tyropitta (cheese and

spinach phyllo-pastry pie – more commonly a bakery takeaway), *marides* (whitebait), *kalamari* (fried squid).

Vegetable dishes – *briam* (baked summer-vegetable mixture, including courgette, aubergine, tomato and potato), *fassolia/fassolaki* (beans in tomato and garlic sauce), 'Greek'/'Village' salad (tomato, cucumber, onion, green pepper and olives topped with feta cheese – a hard, salty, goat's variety).

Fish and seafood dishes – *barbouni* (red mullet), *skoumbri* (mackerel), *xifias* (swordfish, often served shish-kebab style), *garides* (prawns; *garides saganaki* is served in a cheesey casserole), *chtapodi* (octopus). Fish is often barbecued whole. It is priced by weight and, because the Aegean is sorely overfished, can be expensive.

Meat dishes – moussaka (layers of minced meat, aubergine, potato and béchamel sauce), pastitsio/*giouvetsi* (as moussaka, substituting macaroni for potatoes and aubergine), souvlakia (barbecued meat in pitta), keftedes (meatballs), *kokoretsia* (liver and kidneys spit-roasted). The sign '*giro'* indicates meats are spit-roasted. Other common dishes are *kotopoulo* (chicken, usually roasted), *fileto/biftek* (steak – the price will indicate its quality), *sikoti* (liver), *moschari* (veal), *chirino brizola* (pork chop), omelettes, and tomatoes, peppers or aubergines stuffed with rice or minced meat. Pasta and pizza dishes abound, with pizzerias common on most islands.

Desserts – a limited selection usually consisting of the ubiquitous baklava (phyllo pastry and nut *millefeuille* drowned in honey) and yoghurt and honey with fruit. Watermelon and crème caramel also feature quite commonly.

Island specialities – *froutalia* on Tinos and Andros (spicy-sausage omelette); game, when in season, on Naxos; *pseftokeftedes* (tomato rissoles) on Santorini. Syros is famous for its *loukoumi* (Turkish delight) and various nougats but these are bought as shop confectionery, not served in restaurants (see **Best Buys**). Many islands boast their own excellent spicy sausages (e.g. Mykonos and Naxos) and different varieties of cheese which are usually hard and salty. See RESTAURANTS by island, **Eating Out**.

Chora, Folegandros

Health: Before leaving the UK you should obtain form E 111 from the Department of Social Security which entitles you to free medical treatment in Greece (present it to any State doctor you consult who will arrange for you to be exempted from payment). However, standards of health care in Greece are less than adequate and it is also advisable to take out a private health-insurance policy to cover private treatment and the cost of repatriation in the case of serious illness. There are no vaccination requirements unless you are coming from a country where there has been an epidemic.

The most common ailments are self-inflicted by the abuse of sun and alcohol. Angry, red, mosquito-bite swellings are a common high-season sight. By far the best nocturnal mosquito protection is a small machine which slowburns a fume-emitting tablet throughout the night. If you are particularly attractive to mosquitoes avoid perfume and garden restaurants (where the greenery harbours mosquitoes) and spray yourself with a repellent. An anti-mosquito kit can be bought in Britain or on the more popular islands. A less-likely but equally painful threat may be posed by jellyfish, sometimes driven towards the shore by the meltemi (see **Climate**). If you are stung, rub the wound with vinegar from the nearest beach taverna and if problems persist see a chemist or doctor. Motorbike accidents are potentially the most serious hazard. Wear proper shoes and as much clothing as necessary to protect arms and legs should you come off. Request a crash helmet even though you may not get one (see **Bicycle & Motorcycle Hire**). Finally, bear in mind that there are no ambulance services or hospitals on the less-developed islands. However, all the Cyclades (except Sikinos) have at least one doctor and clinic in the summer. See **Chemists**, **Disabled People**, **Emergency Numbers**, **Insurance**.

Hydrofoils: The *Flying Dolphin* hydrofoil fleet services Mykonos, Paros, Naxos, Ios and Santorini during the tourist high season. They are twice as fast as the ferryboats and are twice as expensive. Buy your tickets early as the hydrofoils are very popular but don't expect a smooth ride. They slap rather uncomfortably across the waves but at least don't induce seasickness. See **Boat Services**, **Island-hopping**, **Tourist Information**.

Insurance: You should take out travel insurance covering you against theft and loss of property and money as well as medical expenses, for the duration of your stay. If you intend to hire a motorbike make sure your policy still covers you for accidents. Your travel agent should be able to recommend a suitable policy. See **Bicycle & Motorcycle Hire, Car Hire, Crime & Theft, Driving, Health**.

Ios: 105 sq km. Ios's one historical and cultural claim to fame is the vague possibility that the poet Homer, author of the *Iliad* and the *Odyssey*, was buried here. His last resting place is said to be close to Plakotos in the north, but as this spot is pretty inaccessible, barely

marked and of dubious legitimacy, only the hardiest of pilgrims would come to Ios for this reason. Instead, most people come to Ios to party and to get totally drunk, or that's what it seems. Since the 1950s this pretty island has been attracting young inter-national backpackers and today has the (justifiable) reputation of being the place where 'having a good time' is taken to the limit. Moreover, as the island's three settlements are all adjacent it is difficult to escape the drinking hordes. Nonetheless during the day Chora (see **A–Z**), or Ios Town, is still a lovely, whitewashed maze and the port, Gialos, is also a pleasant spot. Milopotamos beach is a wonderful stretch of sand and though crowded and noisy by day it empties at night to leave a small, peaceful enclave of tavernas (see **IOS-BEACHES**). Travel elsewhere on Ios is difficult, but there is little to see anyway.

Getting there: By ferry, Piraeus (mainland) 11 hr. Direct links: By ferry, Tinos, Santorini, Paros, Naxos, Sikinos, Sifnos; by hydrofoil, Paros, Santorini (coming from Naxos and Mykonos). Getting about: Motorbike hire; no car hire; one frequent bus service between Gialos-Chora-Milopotamos; no taxis. Day trips: Paros, Sikinos, Folegandros. Tourist information: Local Community Authority office opposite the bus stop in Chora. See **IOS**.

Island-hopping: Moving from island to island by ferry or hydrofoil is a good option for those people who tire of a small island after three or four days, or simply want to see as many islands as possible. The heading 'Direct links' at the end of each island description in this section should help you to plan your odyssey. See **Boat Services**, **Hydrofoils**, **Tourist Information**.

Kea: 131 sq km. This lovely green island (which is also known as Keos, Tzia and Zea!) is almost solely the preserve of Greek holiday-makers and gets very crowded at summer weekends. The main resort, Korissia, is a plain fishing village-turned-holiday spot, but it does boast a good beach. Ioulis, the main settlement, is a good example of a working Chora (see **A-Z**) – there are no picturesque, whitewashed houses here – in a lovely hillside situation. Close by is the locally famous Lion of Kea, a 10-m-long, 3-m-tall former guardian of the stadium of ancient Ioulis. Vourkari and Koundouros are the two other main resorts on Kea: both are also former fishing villages blessed with good beaches and now equipped with discos and a nightclub at the Koundouros holiday complex.

Getting there: By ferry, Lavrio (mainland) or Piraeus (mainland) 4 hr. Direct links: Kithnos. Getting about: Motorbike hire; no car hire; frequent but not extensive bus service; some taxis. Tourist information: Korissia.

Kimolos: 35 sq km. Generally regarded as an adjunct to Milos (see **A-Z**), Kimolos is a peaceful, away-from-it-all part of old-world Greece. The small Chora museum, a church and a ruined castle are the only 'sights', but the pretty, crumbling, hillside Chora (see **A-Z**), backed with six windmills, is well worth a visit, particularly at the weekends when you may catch some impromptu dancing. There is a lovely fishing village at Oupa and good, often deserted, beaches at the port, Psathi, and at Aliki and Prassa.

Getting there: 30 min by caïque (a long, narrow, lightweight boat) from Milos. Getting about: One minibus runs from the port to the Chora; boats may be hired to the beaches. Direct links/tourist information: see **Milos.**

Kithnos: 99 sq km. Probably the least interesting of the Cyclades, Kithnos is rocky and barren with nothing out of the ordinary to attract holiday companies. It is, nevertheless, very busy with Athenians in July and August, many attracted by the spa at Loutra. This attractive fishing port-cum-yacht marina is the most popular resort, followed by Merichas and Kanala.

Getting there: By ferry, Lavrio (mainland) or Piraeus (mainland) 4 hr. Direct links: Serifos, Sifnos. Getting about: Motorbike hire; adequate bus service; taxi service; water taxis to the more isolated beaches. Tourist information: Loutra.

Kouros: A term which means, or has come to be applied to, a male statue. On Naxos (see **A-Z**) there are two giant outdoor *kouroi* (the plural of *kouros*) still *in situ* (see **NAXOS-EXCURSION**). Greek *kouroi* date from the 9th-6thC BC and are some of the earliest sculpted studies of man.

Language: If you intend sticking to well-trodden tourist paths, you will encounter few language difficulties – most Greeks in the resorts have a good command of English. However, off the beaten track it will definitely pay you to learn a little Greek. It is also useful to learn how the Greek alphabet translates to the Western alphabet as some road signs and place names are only in Greek. For the sake of politeness at least learn the following expressions: *yassou* (hello/goodbye, general greeting), *kalimera* (good morning), *kalispera* (good evening), *kalinichte* (good night), *parakalo* (please/excuse me), *efcharisto* (thank you).

Laundries: All the major islands have laundries and some have dry-cleaners. Few of these are coin-operated and they rely on staff who may also iron for you. Expect to pay 500-600 Drs per load.

Little Cyclades: A group of sparsely inhabited islands to the south and east of Naxos (also known as the Back Islands). All the islands have excellent sandy beaches, some with tavernas. These are some of the last Greek islands to open up to tourism.
Donoussa: 13 sq km. Around 100 shepherds and fishermen populate four tiny settlements. Café-bars open in the summer.
Epano Koufonissi: 5 sq km. Epano (Upper) Koufonissi is the smallest inhabited island of the Cyclades, with 200-plus fishing folks. It is the most developed of the Little Cyclades.
Schinousa: 8.5 sq km. An island of low hills, lovely bays and around 130 people.

Iraklia (or Heraklia): 17 sq km. The most primitive of the four, it boasts a cave and a ruined castle.
Getting there/Direct links: By ferry from Naxos, Amorgos, Paros.
Getting about: No public transport or vehicles for hire.

Lost Property: If you lose anything, contact the local Tourist Police (see **Police**) and the chances are you will recover it. See **Insurance**.

Markets: Aside from basic fruit-and-vegetable stalls and impromptu fish markets at the harbour, there are no regular markets on the islands.

Milos: 150 sq km. Like Santorini (see **A–Z**), Milos was devastated in prehistoric times by a huge volcanic eruption that sent an enormous chunk of this formerly circular-shaped island to the sea bed, thus creating a huge bay, or caldera. The volcanic legacy is still there to see offshore, with strange rock formations at Kleftiko and the volcanically formed islands of Glaronisia. However, unlike its glamorous eastern volcanic sister isle, Milos – though undoubtedly 'strangely beautiful' (a common description) – has never really embraced tourism. Its lunarlike, quarry-scarred interior (both interesting and ugly) indicates that Milos is still a mining island. It has to be said that the main resort, Adamas, is not 'strangely beautiful' but it does offer the best choice of accommodation and nightlife on the island.
The bay of Adamas has several beaches (many catering for water sports) but the best ones are to be found on the less-accessible south coast. Plaka, or Milos Town, is a typical, pretty Chora (see **A–Z**) with two museums, the archaeological one displaying a copy of the island's most famous treasure, the *Venus de Milo*. This was discovered near here in 1820 amid the ruins of ancient Milos. Also of interest are the well-preserved catacombs nearby at Trypiti, which date from the 1stC AD. Other places worth a look are the small fishing ports of Pollonia, and Klima.
Getting there: By ferry, Piraeus (mainland) 8 hr; by air, Athens 45 min. Direct links: Sifnos, Kimolos, Folegandros. Getting about: Motorbike hire; car hire; regular bus service; taxi service; boats to isolated beaches. Day trips: Sifnos, Kimolos. Tourist information: Adamas.

Hozoviotizza Monastery, Amorgos

Monasteries: Most islands claim at least one monastery or convent, with Naxos (see **A–Z**) boasting six. These vary considerably in appearance from simple church to walled fortress and are frequently situated off the beaten track in order to give their inhabitants peace and solitude. Although nowadays the number of practising souls is dwindling, most monasteries will welcome visitors and some sell home-produced handicrafts. Few have set visiting times so enquire at the nearest tourist information point (see **Tourist Information**). See WHAT TO SEE by island, **Customs**, **Religion**.

Money: The bank is the cheapest place to change money and traveller's cheques, usually levying a small minimum transaction charge and/or a 1% commission. Normal banking hours (0800-1330 Mon.-Fri.) may be extended in the high season in the more popular resorts and some banks open specially for a couple of hours on some evenings just for the exchange of currency. The travel/tourist agencies displaying exchange rates are a more convenient alternative. They are controlled by banking regulations and all offer the same rate as the central banks but charge a commission of 2% on all transactions. Take along your passport when exchanging. Major credit cards are accepted by car-hire firms and by the more up-market shops and restaurants in Mykonos and Santorini but are difficult to use elsewhere. There is a 24-hour Visa cash dispenser in Mykonos Town. See **Crime & Theft**, **Currency**.

Museums: Often overlooked, some of the small Cycladic museums are surprisingly good, particularly those on Mykonos (see **A–Z**). Exhibits are generally captioned in English and are usually very well displayed. Opening hours vary but generally observe the siesta (see **A–Z**). See WHAT TO SEE by island.

Mykonos: 75 sq km. The most famous, or perhaps infamous, of the Cyclades, Mykonos is the busiest and most sophisticated of any of the smaller Greek islands. In recent decades it has also been the gayest of the islands and this has added another dimension to its lively ambience, though latterly it has lost some of its gay-chic appeal. On the negative side overcrowding, overpriced goods and services, and short tempers are common in the high season. If you can go out of season, however, you can't fail to be impressed by Mykonos Town. A picture-postcard port is backed by a beautiful, bewildering, mazy, brilliant-white Chora (see **A-Z**). The Alefkandra 'Little Venice' district by the windmills, and the 'snowy' church of Paraportiani are two highlights. By day, the town evacuates to some of the most splendid beaches in the Aegean (see **MYKONOS-BEACHES 1 & 2**); by night, its beautiful people return to dine at the classiest restaurants (see **MYKONOS-RESTAURANTS**), drink at the coolest cocktail bars and dance to every kind of beat, including traditional Greek music (see **MYKONOS-NIGHTLIFE**). Mykonos need not just be one wild round of hedonistic delights, however: there are some excellent museums (see **MYKONOS-WHAT TO SEE**), the unspoilt village of Ano Mera, and the adjacent island of Delos (see **DELOS-EXCURSION**, **A-Z**) is the greatest archaeological site in the Aegean.

Getting there: By ferry, Rafina (mainland) 5 hr, Piraeus (mainland) 6 hr 30 min; by air, Athens 50 min. Direct links: By ferry, Tinos, Naxos, Paros, Syros; by hydrofoil, Paros (coming from Ios and Santorini); by air, Santorini. Getting about: Motorbike hire; car hire; frequent bus services; taxi services. Day trips: Delos, Tinos, Syros. Tourist information: Mykonos Town. See **MYKONOS**.

Naxos: 428 sq km. Naxos is the largest of the Cyclades and boasts more spectacular scenery, more green and pleasant valleys and more miles of beautiful, unspoilt beaches than any of the other islands. In Naxos Town it also possesses a splendid old-world Chora (see **A-Z**), still mostly residential and unsullied by commercial expediency. Here the island's Venetian heritage looms largest in the shape of the well-preserved Kastro (castle; see **Chora**), although elsewhere among its 40-plus villages there are lots more Venetian mansions to see (see **Venetians**). To explore the island properly and to enjoy all its beaches en route could easily occupy a week. Nightlife on Naxos is quiet compared to the scene on its neighbouring islands but there are discos and several music bars in Naxos Town. There are also some excellent restaurants here (see **NAXOS-RESTAURANTS**) and because of the fertility of the island the standard, staid Greek-taverna menu is enlivened with game, Naxos potatoes, Naxos spicy sausage and other tasty local produce (see **Food**).

Getting there: By ferry, Piraeus (mainland) 6-8 hr, Rafina (mainland) 6 hr 30 min; by air, airport planned to be open for 1992. Direct links: By ferry, Ios, Paros, Amorgos, Little Cyclades, Mykonos; by hydrofoil, Paros (coming from Ios and Santorini). Getting around: Motorbike hire; car hire; frequent bus service; taxi service. Day trips: Paros, Delos, Mykonos. Tourist information: Naxos Town at the waterfront, next to Creperie Bikini. See **NAXOS**.

Newspapers: Foreign papers appear the day after publication on all
the more popular islands (a British daily costs around 200 Drs).
Magazines may take longer.

Nightlife: Aside from discotheques (see **A-Z**) there is little organized
nightlife on the islands outside of festival times. The probability of find-
ing impromptu Greek dancing and singing is slight, but improves as
you get off the beaten track. The excellent Studio 33 on Santorini and
Thalamis on Mykonos are two of the best permanent nightspots for
authentic Greek dancing. See **NIGHTLIFE** by island.

Opening Times: These vary considerably from place to place and
season to season, are subject to frequent changes and can also depend
on the vagaries of the owner or manager. This is especially true of the
discos and nightclubs (see **NIGHTLIFE** by island) which exist purely to
cater for tourists and will open earlier if there is a demand for them or
close when there are too few customers to make it worthwhile staying
open. Greece does not run to a strict timetable! The following times are
very general and are subject to local variation:
Banks – 0800-1330 Mon.-Fri. (some bureaux de change open later).
Bars – 1000-2400 or later.
Post Offices (see **A-Z**) – 0800-2000 Mon.-Fri. (open weekends on some
islands).
Restaurants – 1200-1600, 2000-2400.
Telephone Exchange (OTE) – All open from 0730 Mon.-Fri. On Ios and
Andros they close at 1500 and on other popular islands at 2100 or
2200. Only on Sifnos and Milos is the siesta observed. Mykonos OTE
opens at weekends during the summer peak. See **Siesta**.

Orientation: On arrival at your island go to the local tourist information office (see **A-Z**) and pick up as much free information as possible, including maps. Names of roads are often not marked on maps
and so navigation becomes a fairly hit-and-miss affair, relying on local
landmarks, and even bars and restaurants, as aids. Many of the towns
and islands in the Cyclades have more than one way of spelling their
names and these alternative spellings have been included in their A-Z

listings where necessary: for example, Santorini is also known as Thera and its main town, Fira, can be called, confusingly, Thira.

Paros: 190 sq km. Paros is the crossroads of the Cyclades and the waterfront of Paros Town (Paroikia), its main town and port, constantly throbs with the hustle and bustle of holiday-makers and Greeks trying to get connecting ferries or to pause en route on this lovely island. Behind an unattractive harbour front, Paros Town is typical old-world Cyclades. The remains of a patchwork Kastro (castle) rise above its whitewashed residential Chora (see **A-Z**) dotted with lovely 17thC and 18thC churches. The undulating island is easy and rewarding to travel around, with an abundant supply of beaches (see **PAROS-BEACHES**). It also possesses in Naoussa and Lefkes, two classic Cycladic spots. The former is a picturesque, unspoilt fishing port (see **PAROS-WHAT TO SEE**), the latter a beautiful, decrepit hill village (see **PAROS-EXCURSION**).

Getting there: By ferry Rafina (mainland) 5 hr, Piraeus (mainland) 7 hr; by air, Athens 50 min. Direct links: By ferry, Naxos, Tinos, Sifnos, Syros, Amorgos, Little Cyclades, Ios, Mykonos; by hydrofoil, Naxos, Ios (coming from Santorini), Mykonos. Getting around: Motorbike hire; car hire; regular bus service; taxi service; water taxis to the more isolated beaches. Day trips: Anti Paros, Naxos, Mykonos, Delos. Tourist information: Paros Town, windmill at the port. See **PAROS**.

Passports & Customs: A valid passport (or identity card for some EC visitors) is necessary, but no visa is required for stays of less than three months. If you want to stay longer you must apply to the local police (see **A-Z**) for permission to extend your stay, or to the Aliens Bureau, Alexandras Ave 173, Athens, tel: 01-6468103/7705711, ext. 379. You may be asked to show proof of your financial resources. See **Customs Allowances**.

Petaloudes: See **PAROS-EXCURSION**.

Police: As well as the regular police, who wear green uniforms and deal with crime and traffic offences, there are also the Tourist Police who wear a dark grey-blue uniform and wear badges (in the shape of national flags) to indicate which foreign languages they speak. Their role is to help tourists in trouble and to investigate any complaints about hotels, restaurant prices, etc. See **Crime & Theft**, **Emergency Numbers**.

Post Offices: Every island has a post office open on weekdays from around 0800-2000. On the more popular islands they may also open at weekends. Stamps can be bought at souvenir shops and street kiosks on most islands as well as at the post office.

Public Holidays: Banks and shops close on the following public holidays: 1 Jan. (New Year's Day); 6 Jan. (Epiphany); 25 Mar. (Feast of the Annunciation); Ash Wednesday; Good Friday; Easter Monday; 1 May (Labour Day); 15 Aug. (Assumption Day); 28 Oct. (Ochi Day); 25 Dec. (Christmas Day); 26 Dec. (St. Stephen's Day). See **Events**.

Religion: The national church is the Greek Orthodox, with every tiny hamlet and even individual families on farms possessing their own church. A small number of Catholic churches can also be found, most notably on Syros (see **A-Z, Venetians**). Opening times vary, and many churches are open only during services. Enquire at the tourist information office (see **A-Z**).

See **Churches**, **Customs**, **Monasteries**.

Santorini: 75 sq km. The original circle-shaped island of Santorini (or Thera) was blown in half by a cataclysmic volcanic eruption c.1450 BC. The resultant tidal wave sped over the Aegean at over 200 mph and in minutes wiped out the Minoan civilization on Crete. As around half of old Santorini sank into the sea a new basin, or caldera, was created. The result is one of the world's most dramatic island faces: a sheer red-and-black volcanic-scarred profile which rises 400 m vertically, as high above the water as it is submerged below. The main town, Fira (or Thira), is perched on the cliff face, and although commercialized to meet cruise-line demands it is still very Greek and offers breathtaking views. The lovely town of Oia, too (10 km north of Fira), is built onto the cliff face and is a smaller, less-commercialized version of Fira. Inland, Santorini is predictably barren, although the fertile volcanic-ash soil produces good wines and tomatoes (see **Drinks**, **Food**). There are 13 good-sized villages and the excavations at Akrotiri are well worth a visit (see **SANTORINI-WHAT TO SEE**). Beaches

are grey sand and there are three resorts, developed to an adequate if uninspired standard.

Getting there: By ferry, Piraeus (mainland) 12 hr; by air, Athens 40 min. Direct links: By ferry, Syros, Sifnos, Sikinos, Ios, Anafi, Folegandros; by hydrofoil, Ios (coming from Paros, Naxos and Mykonos); by air, Mykonos. Getting about: Motorbike hire; car hire; frequent bus service; taxi service. Day trips: Ios. Tourist information: No central office, but there are many travel/tourism agencies in Fira (see **Tourist Information**). See **SANTORINI**.

Serifos: 73 sq km. Serifos (or Seriphos) means barren, and this applies not only to the rocky, precipitous landscape but also to tourism on the island. There are some good beaches (but the roads to them are poor), eating out is ordinary and with the exception of a spectacular Chora (see **A-Z**) there is little to see or do here. However, if you are in search of an away-from-it-all place shared with a few Greek tourists, Serifos may be for you.

Getting there: By ferry, Piraeus (mainland) 5 hr. Direct links: Sifnos, Kithnos. Getting about: Motorbike hire; few cars for hire; frequent bus service from Livadi, the main port, to Chora but elsewhere services are infrequent; few taxis for hire. Day trips: Sifnos. Tourist information: Police station in Chora.

Shopping: The only islands where shopping is anything of an attraction are Mykonos and Santorini. Some of the shop windows here would not be out of place in any fashionable European city. Gold and jewellery drip from the boutiques and galleries on the cliff face of Fira, while in Mykonos Town high-fashion wear rules. Both islands cater for an international yachting clientele with bank accounts to match, but there is also plenty that is affordable for lesser mortals. Even if you're not buying, the many small shop galleries on both islands are well worth exploring. Elsewhere, shopping is fairly laid-back, with a typical Cycladic 'High St' (usually a narrow lane) comprising souvenir shops, a bakery, a small, old-fashioned 'supermarket', a leather-goods shop, tourist-clothes shops, and so on. You can haggle, particularly if you are buying more than one item from a store, but this is not so common nowadays on the more fashionable islands. Try it anyway (though not for food or staple goods). See **Best Buys**.

Siesta: This is still very much a part of the Greek way of life. Most shops and businesses shut down between 1400-1700 for an afternoon nap while the tourists are at the beach. Try to avoid the siesta when going to inland villages as they will resemble ghost towns. See **Opening Times**.

Sifnos: 73 sq km. Sifnos (also spelled Siphnos) is the most popular and the most beautiful of the western Cyclades. Green, pleasant and well looked-after, its glistening white houses and emerald valleys have long made it a Greek holiday-makers' favourite. For northern Europeans it is at the stage where tourism development is just beginning. The capital, Apollonia, is a busy, small, unspoilt settlement and nearby is Kastro, the old Chora (see **A-Z**). Further out is the delightful fishing village and beach of Vathy and the resorts of Pharos and Kamares. There are plenty of good sandy beaches on Sifnos and another bonus is the local menu, featuring many island specialities.

Getting there: By ferry, Piraeus (mainland) 8 hr; by air, to Paros or Milos, then by ferry. Direct links: By ferry, Paros, Milos, Ios, Serifos. Getting about: Motorbike hire; car hire; frequent bus service; taxi service. Tourist information: Kamares (by the ferry quay) and Apollonia.

Sikinos: 41 sq km. A small island, 10 nautical miles west of Ios (see **A-Z**), with a population of around 300 people living in the two settlements of the port and the pretty but primitive Chora (see **A-Z**). The island landscape is dramatic – rising to over 550 m – and verdant, the majority of the community being agricultural workers. There are three beaches on the east coast. Basic rooms for rent is the only concession Sikinos makes to tourism.

Getting there/Direct links: By ferry, Piraeus (mainland) 12 hr; other boats make occasional trips from Ios and Santorini. Getting about: One bus from Chora to the port.

Smoking: The Greeks are among the heaviest smokers in Europe and there are few restrictions on public smoking.

Syros: 84 sq km. Syros, the administrative capital of the Cyclades, is dominated by the wealthy town of Ermoupolis (named after Hermes, god of commerce). Ironically for a capital, Ermoupolis looks nothing like any other settlement in the Cyclades, as much of it was built in grand north-European style in the 19thC. Its rise to prominence came as

Ermoupolis town hall

a result of its neutral position in the Greek War of Independence (1812-31) during which it offered sanctuary to many wealthy refugees, including powerful shipbuilding families from Chios. Consequently, after the war Syros became not only the shipbuilding centre of Greece but also an industrial, commercial and cultural focus. Although its dominance was short-lived because of its inability to adapt to new technology, Syros is still one of the few Greek islands involved in the centuries-old Hellenic tradition of shipbuilding and it has retained some of its commercial status. Its former glory and continuing wealth is most manifest in the town hall and square of Ermoupolis (see **SYROS-WHAT TO SEE**), and in the splendid mansions of Posidonia. The faded elegance elsewhere, however, is the clue to the island's recent embracing of tourism, and it may well become a popular resort during the 1990s. It has good, accessible beaches (see **SYROS-BEACHES**), a smattering of nightlife, places of interest (see **SYROS-WHAT TO SEE**) and the atmosphere of real, workaday Greece.

Getting there: By ferry, Rafina (mainland) 4 hr, Piraeus (mainland) 5 hr. Direct links: By ferry, Tinos, Mykonos, Paros, Naxos, Ios, Santorini. Getting about: Motorbike hire; car hire; frequent bus service; taxi service. Day trips: Tinos, Mykonos, Delos. Tourist information: Teamwork Travel, on the waterfront at Ermoupolis (see **Tourist Information**). See **SYROS**.

Taxis: There are taxis on all of the more popular islands, except Ios. They are a good way of getting to beaches which are inaccessible by public transport or of going out for the evening in more comfort and at less cost than hiring a motorbike. You can usually arrange a pick-up time with the drivers, who are mostly reliable. The approximate rate works out at around 80 Drs per km, which can be up to ten times the equivalent bus fare, but still cheap by north European standards. Very few taxis on the islands operate fares on a meter, so agree a price in advance. It is unlikely you will be cheated on the islands, but beware on the mainland (see **Athens**). Note that the taxi may stop to collect other passengers. They will pay a separate fare which, unfortunately, will not mean yours is any less! Water taxis also can take you from your holiday town to the more inaccessible beaches. See **Tipping**.

Telephones & Telegrams: Every island, apart from Sikinos and Anafi, has an OTE (pronounced 'Otay') from where you can make telephone calls and send telegrams. International direct dialling is possible from all the more popular islands but may prove difficult from the rest. To direct dial abroad dial 00 followed by the code for the country (UK: 44, R. of Ireland: 353, USA: 1), then remember to omit the first 0 of the city code. Phones are metered so you pay the cashier after making your call. Telegrams can be sent from OTE offices or by phone. Rates are cheaper after 2100 and at weekends. A three-minute call to Britain will cost around 800 Drs. See **Opening Times**.

Time Difference: Cycladic summer time is two hours ahead of British Summer Time, i.e. when it is midnight in the Cyclades it is 2200 in Britain. The clocks go back one hour in late September and the winter clock remains two hours ahead of GMT.

Tinos: 195 sq km. In 1822 Sister Pelagia of the Convent Kechrovounio, near Tinos Town, had a vision which revealed the whereabouts of a sacred icon of the Virgin and Archangel. After a year of searching the icon was found. Miraculous cures were soon attributed to it and as Greece was fighting and struggling in its War of Independence (1812-31) the icon became a symbol of national salvation. Eventual victory confirmed Tinos as the national contemporary shrine of the Greek Orthodox religion. The focus of attention is the impressive, fortress-like church, Panaghia

Evangelistria (clearly visible from the ferry boat), where rests the holy icon. It is well worth following in the footsteps of the tens of thousands of pilgrims who flock to this 'Greek Lourdes' every year to see the treasures there. The icon itself is heavily laden with votive offerings of precious metals and jewels and small metallic plaques which depict that part of the body for which a heavenly remedy is being requested. The church complex also contains six museums and small galleries. Besides its piety, the island is renowned for its splendid dovecotes (see **A-Z**) which are even more ubiquitous than its 750 churches, and its lovely, unspoilt villages. Some of the best are: the cluster of Kato Klisma, Karkados, Kalloni, Aetofili; the group of Falatados, Mesi, Steni, Potamia; the basket-weaving village of Volax; Kampos, complete with working windmill; Isternia, with marble-arcade streets, a museum of fine arts and a good beach; Kardiane; and Pyrgos (Panormos), renowned as an artists' haven with its School of Fine Art which is open to the public. The best beaches are in the south at Kionia and Ag. Sostis. Tinos Town is a bustling port with a number of lively tavernas and even some cocktail bars and discos.

Getting there: By ferry, Rafina (mainland) 4 hr, Piraeus (mainland) 5 hr. Direct links: By ferry, Andros, Mykonos, Syros. Getting about: Motorbike hire; car hire; frequent bus service; taxi service. Day trips: Mykonos, Andros, Rheneia (Greater Delos; see **Delos**), Delos. Tourist information: Town Hall, Leoforos Megalochoris (on the right-hand side, halfway up the main road to Panaghia Evangelistria). See **Events**.

Tipping: A service charge is always included in the bill at hotels and eating places but it is still customary to leave a tip (of around 5-10%) if the service has been friendly and efficient. If there is a *mikro*, a young boy who helps out, give him a small tip as well. Taxi drivers, tour guides and hairdressers will also expect a tip of around 5-10% for a job well done, while maids and hotel porters are usually given 50-100 Drs.

Toilets: Although some public toilets are quite reasonable, others (particularly the gents') are eye-wateringly disgusting, even in restaurants. Take your own toilet paper, but never flush it away as the narrow-bore plumbing cannot cope with it: instead, place it in the basket provided.

Tourist Information: If you have any specific queries before you go, contact the National Tourist Organization of Greece (NTOG) at 4 Conduit St, London W1R 0DJ, tel: 071-7345997. Many booksellers throughout the country now carry a range of foreign maps, while if you live in London you can buy maps and books from Stanford's, 12-14 Long Acre, London WC2E 9LP. Most islands have some form of official tourist information office and these are stated, by island, in the **A-Z**. If

there isn't an official agency, we state the best office in our opinion. You may have to work hard to get information on the islands: the standard of staff varies considerably and the amount of printed material is negligible. Beware of travel/tourism agencies who try to pass themselves off as official or government centres, as they will invariably just sell you their own tours and services. If there is no office to give independent advice you will just have to shop around for information.

Transport: For details of inter-island movement, see **Boat Services**, **Hydrofoils** and **Island-hopping**. Your choice of which mode of transport to use will probably be determined by the amount of time and money you have available. On the islands themselves motorbike or moped hire is often the best way of getting around (see **Bicycle & Motorcycle Hire**), although car hire may be a better option on a larger island like Naxos (see **Car Hire**). Finally, don't forget that the cheapest and easiest way to move from place to place may be by bus (see **A-Z**) or taxi (see **A-Z**).

Venetians: Only one among a number of invaders, including Minoans, Persians, Romans, Byzantines and Turks, all of whom laid claim to, or took possession of the Cyclades at various times during the islands' surprisingly turbulent and often confusing history. The Venetians controlled the islands for over 350 years and their legacy can be seen particularly clearly in the architecture of Naxos (see **A-Z**) which they held until the middle years of the 16thC. The existence of some small Catholic enclaves among the prevailing Greek Orthodox religion is another remnant of their rule (see **Religion**). See **Dovecotes**.

Walking: Most of the islands will repay dedicated walkers with beautiful flora, particularly in the spring and early summer, and spectacular cliff and hill scenery. Indeed, on some of the less-visited islands shanks's pony is the best (and sometimes only) form of transport. If you do intend walking any distance, remember to wear sun screen and a hat as protection against the sun, carry water and wear good shoes or boots. The only organized walking tours currently on offer are on Andros (see, **A-Z**).

Water: Tap water is generally drinkable on the islands with the possible exceptions of Milos and Syros where it can be very salty. Some islands do suffer from a water shortage during the summer and it is not uncommon for the supply to be turned off during the day.

Water Sports: On most of the developed islands you will find windsurfing, water-skiing and jet-bikes. See BEACHES and note that where 'all water sports' is stated, this means windsurfing, water-skiing and canoeing are all available.

What's On: Ask at the Tourist Information office (see **A-Z**), tourism agencies or even airline offices to see if they have any listings publications – although the chances are they won't, or they will have run out. However, you should be able to get *This Summer in Mykonos* and *Naxos 1991*. See **Events**.

Youth Hostels: These are very rare, due in part to the prolific cheap camping facilities (see **Camping**). In Fira on Santorini (see **A-Z**) there is an authorized hostel close to the centre on the road to Oia and a non-YHA hostel on Eritrou Stavrou. Both charge around 500 Drs per night for a dormitory bed.